EFT

EMOTIONAL FREEDOM TECHNIQUES

"This training program...will teach you how to use this important procedure and many of the subtleties of its application very well."
—David Feinstein, PhD
Author of *Energy Healer's Ethics Handbook*

GET CERTIFIED IN EFT!

EFT certification is a rewarding experience. It opens up new career horizons, as well as personal healing opportunities.

You can obtain CE/CME credits if you're a physician (American Medical Association), nurse (American Nurses Credentialing Commission), psychologist (American Psychological Association) or social worker (NASWB) for Clinical EFT training, which provides a step-by-step process for mastering the "evidence-based" form of EFT.

To enroll click "Certification" at www.EFTUniverse.com

EFT EMOTIONAL FREEDOM TECHNIQUES

EFTUniverse.com

FOR YOUR PROFESSIONAL BOOKSHELF

from

ENERGY PSYCHOLOGY PRESS

The Human Hologram
Living Your Life in Harmony with the Unified Field
By Dr. Robin Kelly

A London-trained physician presents evidence that our physical bodies are perpetually being formed upon an invisible field of information, and that as our consciousness interacts with that field, we can optimize our health.

Softcover, 6" x 9", 256 pages $16.95

Soul Medicine
Awakening Your Inner Blueprint for Abundant Health and Energy
By Norman Shealy, MD, PhD, and Dawson Church, PhD

A neurosurgeon and founder of the American Holistic Medical Association, Shealy teams up with health researcher Dawson Church to present the latest studies showing the healing effects of energy, intention and consciousness.

Softcover, 6" x 9", 296 pages $17.95

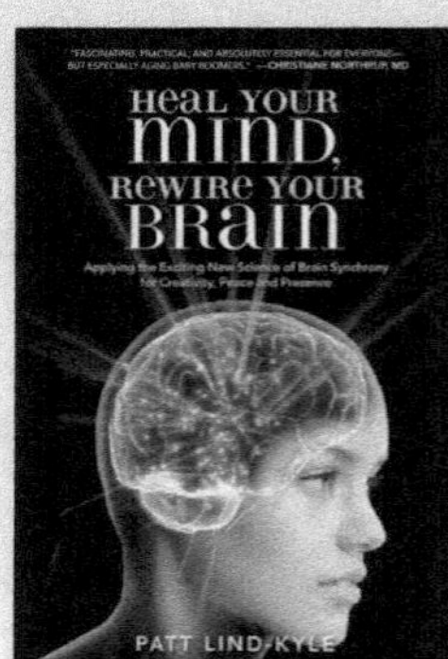

Heal Your Mind, Rewire Your Brain
Applying the Exciting New Science of Brain Plasticity for Creativity, Peace and Presence
By Patt Lind-Kyle, MA

Applies the latest exciting scientific discoveries in a practical, step-by-step program that literally rewires neural connections in the brain for greater happiness.

Hardcover, 6" x 9", 32 Illustrations, 253 pages $26.95

Creating Healing Relationships
Professional Standards for Energy Therapy Practitioners
By Dorothea Hover-Kramer, EdD, RN, DCEP

Written by the co-founder of ACEP, the professional organization for Energy Psychology, this is the first book to seriously address the need for professional standards in the rapidly growing field of energy healing.

Hardcover, 6" x 9", 256 pages $35

Body Eloquence
The Power of Myth and Story to Awaken the Body's Energies
By Nancy Mellon, MFT with Ashley Ramsden

Have you ever had an ache or pain, and wished your body could talk to you and tell you what was wrong? Drawing from mythology, medicine, biology and energetic healing, this book shows the messages that our organs are communicating to us.

Trade Paper, 7" x 10", 15 Illustrations, 260 pages $18.95

Energy Healer's Ethics Handbook
By David Feinstein, PhD, with Donna Eden

This comprehensive, case-oriented guide allows veterans of the field and newcomers alike to work through a wide range of ethical dilemmas before they arise, helping you to prevent professional errors that could hurt you, your clients, and your practice.

Hardcover, 6" x 9", 210 pages $39

ENERGY PSYCHOLOGY PRESS

Order now at EnergyPsychologyPress.com

Energy Psychology
Theory, Research, and Treatment

A Journal of the National Institute for Integrative Healthcare (NIIH.org)

www.EnergyPsychologyJournal.org

Energy Psychology: Theory, Research, and Treatment is a peer-reviewed professional journal dedicated to reporting developments in the field of energy psychology (EP) that are of interest to health care professionals and researchers. It contains original empirical research into the efficacy of EP methods; theoretical, experimental, and basic science papers illuminating the mechanisms of action of EP; clinical insights on the application of EP to various populations, and interfaces with other interventions; book reviews, and abstracts published in other journals that are of relevance to the EP field. Its goal is to further the development of EP as an evidence-based method in the healing sciences. It conforms to the editorial, stylistic, and ethical standards of the American Psychological Association (APA.org).

Energy Psychology: Theory, Research, and Treatment (ISSN 1949-6575) is published biannually (November and May) by Energy Psychology Press, PO Box 222, Petaluma, CA 94953-0222. For customer service or advertising information, contact 707-237-6951 or energypsychologypress@gmail.com.

POSTMASTER: Send address changes to: *Energy Psychology* journal, PO Box 222, Petaluma CA 94953-0222.

YEARLY SUBSCRIPTION RATES: $49.95 per issue, $99.95 per year.

AUTHOR ENQUIRIES: Submit paper copies of proposed papers to *Energy Psychology* journal, PO Box 222, Petaluma CA 94953-0222. Include an e-mail address and phone number for the corresponding author. All submissions should conform fully to the requirements of the *Publication Manual of the American Psychological Association,* sixth edition. Include a cover letter as specified on the "Submissions" link at www.EnergyPsychologyJournal.org, and manuscripts should be prepared in conformity with the other standards published there. Acceptance or rejection will be made via e-mail; paper copies will not be returned. If a submission is accepted for peer review, all subsequent contact will occur via e-mail. Deadline for Spring issue submissions is Jan 15 of each year, and July 15 for Fall issue.

REPRINTS: Back issues are available for $49.95. Reprint ordering information may be found at www.EnergyPsychologyPress.com. To order 100 or more copies of a particular paper, contact energypsychologypress@gmail.com.

www.EnergyPsychologyJournal.org

Contents

May 2024 • Volume 16, Number 1

About

ENERGY PSYCHOLOGY: THEORY, RESEARCH, AND TREATMENT

Energy Psychology (EP) is an evolving and maturing field that is rapidly meeting the standards of proof for "evidence-based" practice. Studies of EP have demonstrated its efficacy for a wide range of psychological and physical problems, from phobias to pain to posttraumatic stress disorder. EP is now being researched in hospital systems such as Britain's National Health Service (NHS), large private hospital chains such as Kaiser Permanente and Sutter Health, and the United States Department of Veterans Affairs (VA). By providing a rigorous, high-quality, peer-reviewed platform for the publication of research results, theory, and clinical insights, this journal provides a forum for the exchange of the key discoveries and ideas that drive the EP field forward.

—Dawson Church, PhD
Editor, *Energy Psychology: Theory, Research, and Treatment*

The journal publishes work in the following areas:

EDITORIAL ESSAYS include guest editorials from some of the best thinkers and researchers in EP today;

ORIGINAL RESEARCH provides empirical evidence for various EP methods;

CLINICAL REPORTS describe the use of EP with challenging conditions and specific populations and provide guidance for empirical research;

INTERFACES WITH OTHER THERAPIES show how EP is typically used in conjunction with other methods, such as cognitive behavior therapy (CBT), mindfulness therapy, addiction counseling, sports psychology, medicine, energy medicine, meditation, and life coaching;

REVIEW ARTICLES are theoretical papers, literature reviews, reports of innovations, and analyses that explore issues from the professional condition of EP to the physiological mechanisms of action of EP;

BOOK REVIEWS cover new and classic EP-related titles;

ABSTRACTS published in other journals relevant to EP are reprinted.

EDITORIAL BOARD

Traveling to the Ultimate Destination

Dawson Church

"We are not going to Bali."

My wife and I looked at each other in surprise as the words emerged from both of us simultaneously.

We had just come to this conclusion in response to a seminar company's invitation to teach a workshop at a luxury resort in Bali. In fact, they wanted me as a speaker so badly they offered to set up a workshop anywhere in the world we desired.

Christine and I have been fortunate in that we have been able to travel widely. Both of us had peripatetic parents who hauled us all over the globe on their journeys. By the time we were teenagers, we'd each visited many countries.

As adults, we always found a way to travel. Even as starving students, we didn't let the lack of funds deter us. Before I got married, I stretched my travel budget by staying at youth hostels and choosing third-class tickets. On a memorable ferry ride in Mexico, I shared the cabin with market vendors carrying cages of chickens and bundles of vegetables on their heads. My wife went to Japan and China with her former husband. I even visited that now-extinct country called the Union of Soviet Socialist Republics. Between us, we've enjoyed most of the Caribbean islands.

When I began training people in energy psychology in the early part of this century, I had an annual standing invitation to teach in France. Christine and I would turn this into a month-long vacation during which we visited other European countries.

By the time we hit 60 years of age, we had traveled to many parts of the globe.

When we shared notes about what remained on our bucket lists, the only place left was Bali.

And here we were, turning down the invitation.

Why?

The reason is we have begun visiting much more exotic places.

We're not making air and hotel reservations to do it. We're not deciding which local sights to see. We're not selecting what to pack and what to leave behind.

The places we are visiting are locations in consciousness. We are traveling to states of awareness far different from the ordinary reality in which most human experience takes place. They are infinitely more enthralling than any destination on a travel agent's itinerary.

The initial goal of meditation is to still the mind. We human beings cannot do this easily. I have been meditating regularly for half a century, rarely missing a day in the past 25 years. Yet each morning when I light the candles, close my eyes, and sit on the cushion, it remains difficult to still my mind.

With practice, the mind does get quieter, though it rarely stops spinning completely. The quieter state gives us a respite from the commentator within. This always-on chatterbox has something to say about everything. It bombards us with its incessant commentary. It criticizes us, second-guesses us, coaches us, scolds us, advises us, ruminates and obsesses about the past.

Hearing this inner cacophony is like being dropped into the middle of an insane asylum, trapped with inmates babbling whatever's on their minds without the filter of sanity or reason.

When we meditate, the voices get a little quieter. As we practice consistently, they get quieter still. There are times when they actually shut up, giving us a glorious expansive inner silence.

At one of my live events, Sally came to the front of the room to talk to me. She told me she had taken my 30-day meditation challenge. Thousands of people all over the world have done this.

I have conducted hundreds of demonstrations of my evidence-based method called EcoMeditation. Afterward I challenge audience members to use it every day—without fail—for 30 days. I ask for a show of hands of those willing to accept this challenge and usually everyone in the audience commits to the 30 days. Sally had been one of those.

"What day are you on now?" I asked Sally.

"I'm on day 147," she reported enthusiastically.

The reason Sally didn't stop after 30 days is that she's become a joy addict. She's grown to enjoy the inner space that EcoMeditation produces such that nothing will deter her from creating the experience daily.

That's the gift of meditation. Practice for just a few days and you'll notice a beautiful new space has opened up inside your head. It's like being in a different country. You explore this new land and find it wonderful. You enjoy this open empty space that was previously filled up with the yammering of the inner critic. That vast expanse is suddenly available.

It's always been there, though it might not have been accessible to you before if your mind was like a cabin your senile uncle has been living in for decades, filled to the brim with knickknacks, mementos, and clutter.

In mental terms, this clutter is the accumulation of a lifetime. It's composed of all the insults, slights, random thoughts, problems, preoccupations, habits, beliefs, grudges, dreams, regrets, reminiscences, ambitions, goals, schemes, trivia, and stories of the past. All these items have so cluttered up the space that the original contours of the cabin are not visible.

Each time you meditate, the collection diminishes. Your emotional attachment to the debris lessens. One day you find yourself at a big, beautiful, open, empty, welcoming warm space. You enjoy mental freedom.

This is the mind you've had all along but weren't able to see because of all the clutter. A new and different way of living your life has opened up. You realize you can make this expensive open space your consistent reality.

As you continue meditating, the clutter-free space gets bigger. You grow to enjoy it. Your mind becomes a temple, rather than an insane asylum. Like Sally, you keep on meditating far longer than your initial commitment because it's wonderful to inhabit this expansive reality.

You've now reached basecamp. That's the first station in the journey of consciousness. Your life usually changes significantly at this point since you are no longer hounded by the voices of the inmates of the insane asylum screeching inside your head.

In the *Yoga Sutras*, the great sage Patanjali describes the goal of spiritual practice as being to "restrain the modifications of the mind." Yogic philosophy teaches that our unmodified state is bliss, but our minds get in the way. They do this by wandering around the piles of clutter. They flit from thought to random thought, distracting us from our natural blissful state. When you're able to restrain this tendency, the mind "flows peacefully inward."

The Sanskrit term for this state is *Samadhi.*

In the *Yoga Sutras*, Patanjali describes nine distinct types of Samadhi. These are nine ecstatic states to which the meditator may travel.

When you're at basecamp, enjoying the open space of a peaceful mind, you begin the journey in consciousness. You might experience Vitarka Samadhi, one of Patanjali's classifications, as you meditate on a candle or the image of a saint. You might soar to heights of bliss and experience another type that Patanjali calls Ananda Samadhi.

You might find yourself drawn to chanting the name of a saint, a mantra, or a sacred sound, and enter Bhava Samadhi.

When you can enter these enchanting states of consciousness, the lure of hauling your body around the planet in search of novel experiences diminishes. When you sit down to meditate, you're traveling to levels of ecstasy beyond the awareness of most members of the human race. A trip to Machu Picchu or Easter Island or Bali doesn't sound nearly as exciting. Even a traveler with a million-dollar budget for the ultimate trip can't get to a destination this replete with grace and ecstasy.

When you reach these levels of Samadhi, you're no longer sitting in an empty room. The space around you is filled with light. You might hear the hum of the universe, or witness celestial colors, or experience emotions for which we don't even have names in English.

Just as Eskimos have 50 different words for "snow" and native Hawaiians have over 200 words for "rain," the Sanskrit language has many different words for what we term "happiness." Like *vishoka*, which means "sorrowless joy." And *ananda*, which means "ecstatic bliss."

In Sanskrit, our conventional conditional happiness is at the bottom of the scale, encapsulated in the word *preyas*, which is used to denote happiness that comes and goes. When you go far beyond preyas and reach a sustained state of happiness, that's termed *sukha*. Vishoka is experienced only in rarified states far above the experience of non-meditators and ananda is experienced by masters.

My wife and I have been sitting in meditation, traveling to these states of Samadhi, and experiencing this extraordinary bliss, every morning. We're traveling to places for which our language doesn't even have words. We don't know where these travels will take us, but we're enthralled by the ride.

We won't be visiting Bali anytime soon.

Optimizing Plant Morphology, Chlorophyll, and Yield Across Plants Through Pranic Healing Techniques: Three Converging Field Studies

K. Nagendra Prasad, World Pranic Healing Foundation, India Research Centre, Mysore, India

Vinu V., World Pranic Healing Foundation

Srikanth N. Jois, World Pranic Healing Foundation

Poornima R., Sri Krishnadevaraya College of Horticultural Sciences, Andhra Pradesh, India

Abstract

The biofield is an energetic field that surrounds living organisms, including humans, animals, and plants. Pranic Healing is a biofield complementary healing practice that aims to balance the energy field, or *prana*, of plants and animals to enhance well-being. Pranic Agriculture (PA) involves replenishing plants with fresh prana to boost development. This study aims to understand the application of PA practices to chili, ridge gourd, and marigold plants grown in field conditions. Chlorophyll content, plant length, stem diameter, root length, days to first flowering, days for first harvest, and yield parameters were compared between pranic-treated and control groups. Chlorophyll content increased in the Pranic group by 26.61% in the ridge gourd plants and 13.64% in the chili; the results were significant ($p < 0.05$) when compared with control. Plant length increased by 22% in chili, 7.4% in ridge gourd, and 3.8% in marigold against the control. Also, the Pranic group had 8% more stem diameter than the control. Root length was found to be significantly increased ($p < 0.05$) in the Pranic group by 44% in chili and 38.46% in ridge gourd. The Pranic group had earlier flowering and earlier harvest dates than the control group. When comparing crop yield, Pranic yielded more in chili (16.71%), ridge gourd (5.85%), and marigold (30.67%) than the respective control groups. This validates that Pranic Agriculture has the potential to increase crop productivity significantly.

Keywords: flowering, harvest, prana, Pranic Healing, Pranic Agriculture, root length, yield

K. Nagendra Prasad, PhD, is senior research consultant at the World Pranic Healing Foundation, India Research Centre in Mysore, Karnataka, India. **Vinu V., MSc.,** is a research associate at the World Pranic Healing Foundation. **Srikanth N. Jois, PD,** is research head at the World Pranic Healing Foundation. **Poornima R., PhD,** is assistant professor in the Department of Plant Physiology, Sri Krishnadevaraya College of Horticultural Sciences, Ananthapuramu, Andhra Pradesh, India. **Correspondence: Srikanth N. Jois, PD,** World Pranic Healing Foundation India Resarch Center, No. 44, First Floor, 4th Main, 1st Cross, Sarswarthipuram, Mysore 570009, Karnataka, India; email: research@pranichealing.co.in. **Disclosure:** The authors declare no conflict of interest.

Energy treatment is an emerging field of study for increasing agricultural productivity. It causes physiological and biochemical changes that reflect plant growth and development processes, eventually improving yield and produce quality. Measurable energy treatments include magnetic, sound, heat, and light (Feinstein, 2022). For over 10,000 years, farmers have used invisible energy, nonmaterial, and spiritual techniques such as meditation, mantra farming, spiritual farming, agnihotra (Parrott, 2021), Pranic Agriculture (Prasad & Jois, 2021), and the biofield

(Lee & Wu, 2019). Though typically unmeasured, these are considered traditional methods to promote crop growth and productivity.

The term "biofield" encompasses noncontact or intentional healing energy interactions among organisms, reflecting various energies influencing living organisms, including their self-regulation processes. These energies may include electromagnetic fields, subtle energy, biophotons, and quantum processes. Biofields are integral to comprehending energy-based therapies. Research has examined the biological effects of biofields across diverse multicellular organisms, ranging from proteins and bacteria to animals and plants (Church, 2023).

Pranic Healing is a biofield practice promoting holistic approaches to wellness that acknowledge the existence of subtle energies within and around the body. Pranic Healing, founded by Filipino Master Choa Kok Sui, involves the manipulation and balance of *prana*, or life energy, to facilitate physical, emotional, and mental healing. Practitioners use specific techniques to cleanse, energize, and balance the biofield (Sui, 1992b).

Pranic Agriculture (PA) entails the transmission of prana to plants to stimulate growth. Prana is the vital energy mentioned in Yogic texts, the Upanishads, and Ayurveda, and it is required to keep the body alive and healthy (Sui, 1992b). It is also referred to as *chi* in Chinese, *ki* in Japanese, or, in general, biofield or subtle energy. There are three major sources of prana, namely, ground prana, sun prana, and air prana. Water absorbs prana from the ground, sunlight, and air. Trees and plants absorb prana from the ground, sun, and air (Sui, 1992b). This prana can be captured surrounding a leaf using Kirlian photography (Pisotska et al., 2020).

Pranic Agriculture, which originated in Southeast Asia, aims to enhance plant growth by manipulating energy fields in soil and seeds. It utilizes Pranic Healing techniques and requires completion of a training program, which is offered globally for those interested in this alternative approach. PA cannot be used as a substitute for farming; rather, it is a supplement and can be implemented in any agricultural field with no additional expense. Plants can be treated with PA to promote faster growth, increase yield, and improve the physical, nutritional, sensory, and storage qualities of fruits (Rainer, 2015). Recent studies have revealed that employing PA can increase seedling vigor, crop yield, and sensory and storage qualities of crops (Poornima et al., 2021a; Prasad & Jois, 2021; Yathindra et al., 2017).

When the pranic energy is applied to the seeds, the energy level in the seeds increases, resulting in a greater germination percentage. These result in more energy supplied to the cells during cell division and elongation, growth, and differentiation, resulting in enhanced growth of plants, root length, and crop yield (Poornima et al., 2021b). By applying pranic energy to cabbage, a polymorphism of 22% was obtained between the Pranic and the control groups. This indicates there is substantial variability between the two groups. The externally applied pranic energy might have acted as a stimulus to the plants and might have brought about changes at DNA and cellular levels (Poornima et al., 2021a).

Seedlings of wheat and peas germinated faster when treated with chi energy against the control (Bai et al., 2000). Biofield-treated lettuce and tomato plants yielded 43% and 31% more when compared to untreated plants (Shinde et al., 2012). Enhanced germination, an increase in shoot and root length, and crop yield were noticed in groundnut (peanut) and wheat when treated with meditation (Pandey et al., 2015). In lettuce and bok choy plants, higher vegetative growth and increase in chlorophyll contents were noticed in biofield-treated plants when compared with control (Lee & Wu, 2019).

Chi energy could impact some changes in germination-related genes. It was also observed that chi energy can change the cellular structures of mitochondria and can influence cell metabolism, affect gene expression, enzyme activity, and nucleotide polymerization. Application of chi energy increased the rate of cellular growth and division, and increased ATPase (enzyme) activity during germination of the dividing cells (Bai et al., 2000).

Objectives

The objectives of the current work are to study the influence of Pranic Agriculture on growth, flowering, and fruiting of chili, ridge gourd, and marigold plants.

Methods

Experimental Site

This study was carried out at the College of Horticulture, Yelwala, Mysore, India, in the year 2019 under field conditions. The location coordinates were 12.38015N, 76.52426E. Chili (*Capsicum annuum* L.), ridge gourd (*Luffa acutangular* variety Naga), and marigold (*Tagetus erecta* L. variety Tennis ball) seeds were procured from the local market in Mysore, India.

Pranic Treatment

The pranic treatment involved the transfer of prana to seed, cocopeat, soil, and crop, using a standard protocol. A trained pranic healer with more than 10 years of experience applied Pranic Healing techniques six times for 15 minutes each. The treatment involved using green prana to remove used-up energies from the seeds, cocopeat (coconut peat), and soil. "Used-up energies" refers to pranic energy that has become stagnant or depleted of its vitality. Imagine it like a used battery; it still has some energy but not enough to function effectively. Pranic Healing removes used-up energies, which can accumulate in the aura and energy field, and supplies fresh prana. Similar to how colored light therapy uses different wavelengths for various purposes, Pranic Healing uses colored pranas to target specific areas or issues. Pranic Healing theory suggests that the body and its energy field respond to specific energetic frequencies associated with different colors. After removing the contaminated energies, the seeds, cocopeat, and soil were then energized with electric violet prana.

Pranic treatment was given to the soil of the Pranic group three weeks before sowing (Sui, 1992a). The seed, cocopeat, soil, and crop with no Pranic Healing treatment are referred to as the control group. Seeds are treated with pranic energy and sown in the nursery trays filled with cocopeat, which has been treated with pranic energy and another set without treatment. These trays are maintained separately in a greenhouse. Both sets were cultivated in a greenhouse for up to 25 days before being transplanted to their respective Pranic and control field plots for study.

While the seedlings were establishing in the greenhouse, the Pranic Healing land was treated with pranic energy, and another set of land was kept as control. The lands were 50 feet apart. Transplantation was carried out in the treated plots (0.2 hectares each) for each crop. Both experimental plots (Pranic and control) were made of red loam soil with equal environmental conditions, and drip irrigation was used to hydrate them. Before transplanting the seedlings, the required dose of FYM (farm yard manure; 15–20 tons/ha) is applied to the field. Chemical fertilizer at the rate of 150:75:75 kg/ha (NPK [nitrogen, phosphorous, potassium]) was applied in two split doses or whenever it was required. Weeding and other required agricultural activities were performed on a regular basis.

Field Observations

Uniform and healthy seedlings 25 days old were transplanted from the greenhouse to the main field and allowed to establish themselves. Morphological growth traits such as plant height (cm), stem girth (cm), and root length (cm) were measured using a measuring tape. Flowering trait parameters like days taken for first flowering and first harvest were recorded when flower and fruit emergence was noticed. Yield traits such as flower/fruit length (cm), flowers/fruit weight (g), number of flowers/fruits per plant, flower/fruit girth (cm), and yield per acre (t [ton]) were recorded after the harvest. To maintain objectivity and integrity in the results, data collection was carried out by investigators from the College of Horticulture in Mysore.

Chlorophyll Content

Total chlorophyll content (mg/g) of crop leaves was measured using the dimethyl sulphoxide (DMSO) method (Shoaf & Lium, 1976).

Statistical Analysis

Crop morphological and yield data were analyzed from 10 samples for each treatment. The *t*-test was used for statistical analysis, and the findings are given as mean SD, with significance set at $p < 0.05$. The difference between the values of treatment and control is computed and given as a percentage.

Results

Effect of Pranic Agriculture on Chili

Chlorophyll content (mg/g) of the Pranic group was higher (4.25 ± 0.26) than in the control (3.74 ± 0.20). Similarly, the height and root length of pranic-treated chili plants were greater than control and the results were significant ($p < 0.05$; see Table 1). Root length, plant height, and chlorophyll content were higher by 43.98%, 21.9%, and 13.6%, respectively, when compared with control. The stem diameter of the Pranic group plants was also higher than the control, but the results were nonsignificant. Flowering in the Pranic group was earlier (24 days) when compared to control (25 days). As a result, fruit harvesting was

Table 1. *Influence of Pranic Treatment on Chlorophyll Content, Plant Growth, Flowering, and Yield of Chili*

Traits	Control	Pranic
Chlorophyll content (mg/g)	3.74 ± 0.20	4.25 ± 0.26* (+13.64%)
Plant height (cm)	43.53 ± 3.54	53.08 ± 6.41* (+21.94%)
Stem girth (cm)	0.99 ± 0.17	1.07 ± 0.10 (+8.08%)
Root length (cm)	13.28 ± 2.87	19.12 ± 2.90* (+43.98%)
Days to first flowering	25.36 ± 1.99	24.58 ± 2.59 (–3.08%)
No. of days taken for first harvest	46.75 ± 0.95	46.25 ± 1.89 (–1.07%)
No. of fruits/plant	22.3 ± 4.81	25.8 ± 2.66 (+15.70%)
Fruit length (cm)	8.46 ± 1.40	9.31 ± 0.87 (+10.05%)
Fruit girth (cm)	1.06 ± 0.10	1.18 ± 0.20 (+11.32%)
Fruit weight (g)	5.56 ± 0.60	6.47 ± 0.62* (+16.37%)
No of seeds/fruit	51.1 ± 4.98	64.5 ± 10.5* (+26.22%)
Yield/acre (t)	12.21 ± 0.81	14.25 ± 0.81* (+16.71%)

Note: All data presented in Mean ± SD ($n = 10$) and *$p < 0.05$ (significant) as compared to control group. + = % increase, – = % decrease, when compared to control group.

first noticed in the Pranic group against the control. Other parameters including number of fruits per plant, fruit length, and fruit diameter were all higher in the Pranic group when compared to control. The number of seeds per fruit and fruit weight was significantly higher in Pranic (64.5 and 6.47 g) when compared to control (51.1 and 5.56 g). Pranic treatment had 26.22% and 16.37% improvement in number of seeds per fruit and fruit weight over the control. The number of seeds per fruit and fruit weight was significantly increased by pranic treatment; these are the main yield-contributing traits. The major qualities responsible for the pungency of chili are the number of seeds, which was increased by Pranic Healing. Yield per acre was also found statistically higher in pranic treatment by 16.7% when compared with the control plot. Pranic treatment recorded 14.3 ton yield per acre whereas control gave 12.2 tons (Poornima et al., 2021b).

Effect of Pranic Agriculture on Ridge Gourd

Chlorophyll content (mg/g) of the ridge gourd in the Pranic group was greater (3.14 ± 0.38), than in the control plants (2.48 ± 0.22) and the difference was significant ($p < 0.05$; see Table 2). Vine length was higher in Pranic against the control, higher by 7.46%, but the results were nonsignificant. An increase of 38.46% in root length and stem girth by 8% was observed in Pranic versus control and the results were found to be significant ($p < 0.05$). Female flowering was first found in Pranic (38.73 ± 2.58 days), while control took an additional day to flower (39.1 ± 2.36 days). This helped in early fruit harvest in the Pranic group when compared to control and the results were found to be significant ($p < 0.05$). Other yield parameters—number of fruits/plant, fruit length, fruit diameter, and fruit weight—were all higher in Pranic, but the results were nonsignificant. The yield in the control group was lower (12.66 ± 1.63 t) than in the Pranic group (13.40 ± 1.63 t) by 5.85% (Poornima et al., 2020a).

Effect of Pranic Agriculture on Marigold

Marigold in the pranic-treated group had increased chlorophyll content, which was 9.65% higher than in the control group (Table 3). Plant spread (cm^2) at 60 days was found to be significantly higher ($p < 0.05$) in the Pranic group (42.34 ± 3.11) when compared with the control (36.38 ± 3.38). Plant spread in Pranic increased by 16.38% more than the control. Furthermore, the number of branches in the Pranic group was found to be significantly increased versus the control. Root length and plant length were higher in Pranic, but the results were nonsignificant. Flowering was first noticed in the Pranic group (64.1 ± 6.58 days), while in control it took more days to flower (68.26 ± 7.86 days) and the difference was found to be significant. Significant results were also noticed

Table 2. *Influence of Pranic Treatment on Chlorophyll Content, Plant Growth, Flowering, and Yield of Ridge Gourd*

Traits	Control	Pranic
Chlorophyll content (mg/g)	2.48 ± 0.22	3.14 ± 0.38* (+26.61%)
Vine length (m)	5.63 ± 0.87	6.05 ± 0.33 (+7.46%)
Stem girth (cm)	6.0 ± 0.77	6.48 ± 0.75* (+8%)
Root length (cm)	12.87 ± 1.71	17.82 ± 0.67* (+38.46%)
Days to first female flowering	39.1 ± 2.36	38.73 ± 2.58 (–0.95%)
No. of days taken for first harvest	61.5 ± 3.0	55.25 ± 3.86* (–10.16%)
No. of fruits/plant	7.50 ± 1.98	7.70 ± 1.82 (+2.67%)
Fruit length (cm)	45.68 ± 4.36	45.23 ± 2.63 (–0.99%)
Fruit girth (cm)	4.95 ± 0.56	4.70 ± 0.36 (–5.05%)
Fruit weight (g)	459.74 ± 21.87	468.62 ± 69.56 (+1.93%)
Yield/acre (t)	12.66 ± 1.63	13.40 ± 1.63 (+5.85%)

Note: All data presented in Mean ± SD ($n = 10$) and *$p < 0.05$ (significant) as compared to control group. + = % increase, – = % decrease, when compared to control group.

Table 3. *Influence of Pranic Treatment on Chlorophyll Content, Plant Growth, Flowering, and Yield of Marigold*

Traits	Control	Pranic
Chlorophyll content (mg/g)	3.42 ± 0.28	3.75 ± 0.10 (+9.65%)
Plant length at 60 DAT (cm)	41.42 ± 6.80	43 ± 7.64 (+3.81%)
Plant spread at 60 DAT (cm^2) (E-W)	36.38 ± 3.38	42.34 ± 3.11* (+16.38%)
No. of branches	11.06 ± 2.39	12.60 ± 2.39* (+13.92%)
Root length (cm)	11.26 ± 2.92	14.02 ± 3.09 (+24.51%)
Days to first flowering	68.26 ± 7.86	64.1 ± 6.58* (–6.09%)
No. of days taken for first harvest	93.25 ± 1.71	91.25 ± 3.5 (–2.14%)
No. of flowers/plant	58.26 ± 6.57	72.10 ± 9.66* (+23.76%)
Flower diameter (cm)	4.87 ± 0.32	5.77 ± 0.30* (+18.48%)
Yield/plant (g)	449.7 ± 75.46	587.60 ± 83.34* (+30.67)
Yield/acre (t)	4.66 ± 0.81	6.09 ± 0.81* (+30.69%)

Note: All data presented in Mean ± SD ($n = 10$) and *$p < 0.05$ (significant) as compared to control group. DAT = days after transplantation; + = % increase, – = % decrease, when compared to control group.

in the number of flowers per plant, flower diameter, and yield per plant in the Pranic group; increased by 23.76%, 18.48%, and 30.67% respectively, against the control. Yield per acre in control was lesser (4.66 ± 0.81 t), while in Pranic it was increased by 30.69% (6.09 ± 0.81 t) and the results were found to be significant (Poornima et al., 2020b).

Discussion

Plants treated with PA were found to have higher plant growth, increased stem diameter and root length, earlier flowering, and higher yield. Water, when treated with Pranic Healing was found to have lower contact angle and lower surface tension (Ananthakeshava et al., 2021). Lower surface tension of water aids in enhanced nutrient absorption by plants due to improved soil penetration and soil wetting, increased capillary action facilitating better nutrient movement, improved root absorption, and enhanced nutrient transport within the plant, thus contributing to better plant growth (Hallett, 2008). PA plants have increased stem diameter. An increase in stem diameter in crops is directly related to higher crop yield, as it reflects greater vascular tissue development, allowing for improved nutrient and water transport, enhanced structural support for increased biomass production, and potentially higher photosynthetic capacity, all contributing collectively to higher yield potential (Chang et al., 2022; Yang et al., 2022). Also, pranic-treated plants had longer root lengths. The longer the root length, the higher nutrition absorption by the plants because of the presence of more root hairs (Fageria & Moreira, 2011) and hence higher plant yield.

Pranic agricultural practices promote early flowering and fruiting, resulting in expedited harvests, potentially increasing farmers' profitability by enabling shorter production cycles and quicker time to market. Embracing Pranic Agriculture offers farmers an array of significant benefits, enriching their income potential and bolstering agricultural sustainability. By incorporating pranic principles into their farming methods, farmers unlock a holistic approach that optimizes plant growth, boosts crop yields, and fortifies resilience against environmental challenges. This comprehensive strategy not only enhances productivity but also ensures the production of superior-quality crops, commanding premium prices in the market. Furthermore, Pranic Agriculture provides sustainable alternatives by reducing reliance on chemical inputs and advocating for eco-friendly farming practices. With a focus on achieving energetic equilibrium and harmonizing the agricultural ecosystem, Pranic Agriculture charts a path for farmers to elevate their livelihoods while contributing to the long-term sustainability of agriculture.

This study provides the usefulness of PA in enhancing ridge gourd, chili, and marigold plant growth.

Conclusion and Future Perspectives

Pranic Agriculture can have a significant impact on agriculture to increase crop yields, by increasing plant growth, stem diameter, and root length and quickening the time to flowering and fruit harvest. PA can be a supportive farming system to the existing conventional agricultural methods in achieving sustainability, food security, and quality for farmers. The use of PA, in addition to regular farming practices, helps farmers harvest good quality and quantity produce at an earlier date. As a result, farmers will, in turn, obtain premium prices for their produce, with the benefit of increased income. The application of PA is easy and does not require specialized techniques. Any interested farmer can be trained to adopt PA in their field. The projected pranic energy affects the plant physiology and brings about significant morphological changes in the plants. The mechanisms behind this are the major thrust area for further investigations.

Acknowledgments

We thank Master Choa Kok Sui, the founder of modern Pranic Healing for imparting the precise knowledge of Pranic Agriculture; trustees of World Pranic Healing Foundation, India, for encouragement, support, and funding the study; Dr. Yathindra and the Dean of the College of Horticulture, Mysore, for their generous technical support to conduct the study; and Dr. Rainer K., Mr. Papanna, and Ms. Shalini for their sincere contributions.

Funding

World Pranic Healing Foundation, India.

References

Ananthakeshava, I., Srikanth, N. J., Prasad, K. N., & Vinu, V. (2021). Reduction in surface tension of water due to Pranic Healing. *Indian Journal of Science and Technology, 14*(26), 2175–2179. doi:10.17485/IJST/v14i26.488

Bai, F. C., Sun, Z., Liu, J., Shen, Y., Shen, R., Ge, C., ... Shi, Y. (2000). Seeds induced to germinate rapidly by mentally projected 'qi energy' are apparently genetically altered. *American Journal of Chinese Medicine, 28*(01), 3–8. doi:10.1142/S0192415X00000039

Chang, W., Chen, H., Jiao, G., Dou, Y., Liu, L., Qu, C., & Lu, K. (2022). Biomolecular strategies for vascular bundle development to improve crop yield. *Biomolecules, 12*(12), 1772. doi:10.3390/biom12121772

Church, D. (2023). Measuring the effect of Clinical Emotional Freedom Techniques (EFT) treatment for depression using a seed bioassay: A randomized controlled trial. *Psychology, 14*(11), 1687–1697. doi:10.4236/psych.2023.1411098

Fageria, N. K., & Moreira, A. (2011). The role of mineral nutrition on root growth of crop plants. *Advances in Agronomy, 110*, 251–331. doi:10.1016/B978-0-12-385531-2.00004-9

Feinstein, D. (2022). The energy of energy psychology. *OBM Integrative and Complementary Medicine, 7*(2), 1–28. doi:10.21926/obm.icm.2202015

Hallett, P. D. (2008). A brief overview of the causes, impacts and amelioration of soil water repellency—a review. *Soil and Water Research, 3*(1), S21–S28.

Lee, C. T., & Wu, H. C. (2019). Effect of biofield treatment on growth and physiology of hydroponically grown lettuce and bok choy plants. *Agrivita Journal of Agricultural Sciences, 41*(3), 395–404. doi:10.17503/agrivita.v41i3.2337

Pandey, S. T., Verma, O., Pandey, D. S., Gill, S., Patel, J. C., Patel, G. N., & Thakur, D. M. (2015). Yogic farming through Brahma Kumaris Raja Yoga Meditation: An ancient technique for enhancing crop performance. *Asian Agriculture History, 19*(2), 105–122.

Parrott, N. (2021). *Subtle agroecologies: Farming with the hidden half of nature*. CRC Press, Taylor and Francis. doi:10.1201/9780429440939

Pisotska, L., Yevdokymenko, N., Stetsula, N., & Stakhiv, V. (2020). Kirlianography of bioelectric properties in plants. *Human Health: Realities and Prospects. Monographic Series, 5*(Ch. 13), 161–172. Retrieved from http://repo.dma.dp.ua/id/eprint/6094

Poornima, R., Prasad, K. N., Yathindra, H. A., & Jois, S. N. (2020a). Influence of pranic agriculture on morphological traits, chlorophyll content and genetic polymorphism of ridge gourd (*Luffa acutangula* L. Roxb.) assessed by RAPD marker analysis. *Agrivita Journal of Agricultural Science, 42*(3), 521–532. doi:10.17503/agrivita.v42i3.2715

Poornima, R., Prasad, K. N., Yathindra, H. A., & Jois, S. N. (2020b). Influence of pranic agriculture technique on growth and yield of marigold, *Tagetus eracta. Bioscience Biotechechnology Research Communication, 4,* 2001–2007. doi:10.21786/bbrc/13.4/55

Poornima, R., Prasad, K. N., Yathindra, H., & Jois, S. N. (2021a). Influence of pranic agriculture as a complementary treatment on yield and RAPD polymorphism in cabbage (*Brassica oleracea* L.). *Plant Cell Biotechnology and Molecular Biology, 22*(33–34), 265–273. Retrieved from https://ikprress.org/index.php/PCBMB/article/view/6376

Poornima, R., Prasad, K. N., Yathindra, H., & Jois, S. N. (2021b). Influence of pranic agriculture in enhancing growth and yield of Chilli (*Capsicum annuum* L.) and its genetic analysis. *Egyptian Journal of Agriculture Research, 99*(3), 242–247. doi:10.21608/EJAR.2021.90527.1135

Prasad, K. N., & Jois, S. N. (2021). Effect of pranic agriculture treatment on growth of cluster beans (*Cyamopsis tetragonoloba* L.). *Indian Journal of Agriculture Research, 55*(3), 359–363. doi:10.18805/IJARe.A-5509

Rainer, K. (2015). *Pranic agriculture, comparative trials from Germany, India and Columbia*. Retrieved from https://pranichealingresearch.com/index.php/2023/11/19/pranic-agriculture-comparative-trials-from-germany-india-and-colombia

Shinde, V., Sances, F., & Patil, S. (2012). Impact of biofield treatment on growth and yield of lettuce and tomato. *Australian Journal of Basic Applied Science, 10*(6), 100–105.

Shoaf, W. T., & Lium, B. W. (1976). Improved extraction of chlorophyll a and b from algae using dimethyl sulfoxide. *Limnology and Oceanography, 21*(6), 926–928. doi:10.4319/lo.1976.21.6.0926

Sui, C. K. (1992a). *Advanced Pranic Healing: A practical manual on color Pranic Healing*. Bangalore, India: Institute of Inner Studies Publishing Foundation.

Sui, C. K. (1992b). *The ancient science and art of Pranic Healing*. Bangalore, India: Institute of Inner Studies Publishing Foundation.

Yang, Y., Dong, S., Miao, H., Liu, X., Dai, Z., Li, X., & Zhang, S. (2022). Genome-wide association studies reveal candidate genes related to stem diameter in cucumber (*Cucumis sativus* L.). *Genes, 13*, 1095. doi:10.3390/genes13061095

Yathindra, H. A., Srikanth, N. J., Prasad, N. K., & D'Souza, L. (2017). Influence of pranic agriculture on germination, flowering and yield of European cucumber. *Ecology Environment & Conservation, 23*(3), 1770–1773.

Energy Psychology for Social Anxiety and Erythrophobia: A Case Study

Annick Pujol, Paris, France

Abstract

Background: The intense fear of blushing in public (erythrophobia) is part of the spectrum of social anxiety that affects between 3% and 13% of the population. This phobia can be very debilitating for those who suffer from it. It may stem from a difficult childhood marked by educational attitudes based on shame and humiliation as well as repeated traumatic experiences.
Objective: The aim here is to explain in detail how the energy psychology techniques Clinical EFT (the manualized form of Emotional Freedom Techniques) and Energetic Memory Reconsolidation Therapy function in practice, as applied to "Jeanne," a young woman suffering from social anxiety and erythrophobia following a chaotic start in life.
Method and setting: The therapeutic plan was drawn up on the theoretical basis of the scientific literature on energy psychology, which has produced convincing results in the treatment of trauma and anxiety. The therapy was threefold: (a) learning to manage anxiety autonomously using Clinical EFT, (b) trauma treatment using Energetic Memory Reconsolidation Therapy, and (c) psycho-education. Jeanne had a total of 15 sessions, two of which are detailed here to illustrate the work. At the start of each session, the SUD (Subjective Units of Distress) scale was used to rate the level of blushing anxiety (the scale ranges from 0 to 10, with 0 being no distress and 10 being the most imaginable).
Results: The level of anxiety decreased from 9/10 to 3/10 between the first and last sessions. In addition, the number of problem situations encountered (blushing having generated negative emotions) dropped from 5 per week to 0 per week between the beginning and end of therapy. Jeanne's goal of not blushing at her wedding was achieved. She was able to experience the event without worrying about or even thinking about the anxiety.
Conclusion: Psychotherapy based on energy techniques enabled me to treat Jeanne's social anxiety and erythrophobia in depth by targeting the sources while giving her access to an emotional regulation tool to use independently: Clinical EFT.

Keywords: erythrophobia, fear of blushing, social anxiety, Emotional Freedom Techniques, Clinical EFT, Memory Reconsolidation, Matrix Reimprinting

Annick Pujol, a psychologist and psycho-practitioner in energy and cognitive-emotional techniques, trained at the Institut Francophone de Psychothérapie Émotionnelle et Cognitive (IFPEC) and works in private practice, mainly with patients suffering from anxiety disorders. **Correspondence:** Annick Pujol, 8 rue Edmond Roger, 75015 Paris, France; email: annickpujol.energetique@gmail.com. **Disclosure:** The author receives income from therapy consultations that may or may not include the methods covered in this article.

Erythrophobia is defined as the intense fear of blushing in public and is part of the social anxiety spectrum. Sufferers are progressively overcome by the shame of blushing and the anxiety that goes with it, leading them to avoid social situations. Their social life becomes restricted and their quality of life can be severely impaired. Erythrophobia can therefore be very disabling.

Although patients with erythrophobia often say they have tried several types of therapy to no avail and continue to suffer (Laederach-Hofmann et al., 2002), there is little scientific research on the subject. However, a study of 40 people diagnosed with erythrophobia has begun to provide some insight into the mechanisms of this disorder. The authors detected abnormal functioning of the autonomic nervous system under mental stress in these people, compared with a group of healthy people, concluding that "patients with erythrophobia do not seem to be able to reduce sympathetic and parasympathetic tone to comparable values as normal subjects do or up-regulate it as an effect of a more pronounced counterregulation in mental stress conditions" (Laederach-Hofmann et al., 2002). This result indicates that, to be effective, therapies should focus on modifying this stress response.

EFT (Emotional Freedom Techniques) is a mind-body technique that involves tapping acupressure points with the fingers while mentally exposing oneself to a stressful memory, event, or thought. More than 155 scientific studies have demonstrated the effectiveness of this method, particularly in reducing stress and anxiety, and in treating phobias, depression, and posttraumatic stress disorder (PTSD). EFT acts directly and rapidly on the autonomic nervous system, reducing levels of stress hormones such as cortisol (Stapleton et al., 2020). By acting on the autonomic nervous system, EFT could have a positive effect on erythrophobic patients whose nervous systems are dysfunctional.

This is why I chose EFT as the basic technique for conducting therapy with "Jeanne," a client who had been suffering from erythrophobia for several years. This article details the therapeutic approach.

Jeanne's Case

At the start of her therapy, Jeanne encountered three pervasive problems in her daily life. First, she suffered from facial blushing whenever she was in public, whether with friends or strangers. Second, she felt lost in her desire to change careers and no longer knew what she really wanted to do. She felt that she was spreading herself too thin, running in all directions, and wanted to control everything, but she couldn't seem to slow down. Third, in general, she was always ashamed of not being perfect.

At the end of the first session, after taking an anamnesis (the dialogue that precedes any clinical examination and enables the practitioner to reconstruct the life history of the client and those around her) and identifying her three main problems, Jeanne chose to work on her frantic running and her inability to slow down. However, she didn't seem very convinced about working on this. At the next session, she explained that the real problem was the shame of not being perfect, of disappointing, of not measuring up, which was reflected in her blushing. She wanted to work on getting rid of this shame. The goal was clear: to stop blushing in social situations and, in particular, at her wedding in nine months' time.

A Seemingly Enviable Life

Jeanne is 28 and lives with her partner. She is a graduate of a Grande École (an elite French institution of higher education for professional or technological training) and currently works freelance in professional training while preparing to transition to the educational field. She's a sparkling, well-groomed young woman with a big smile. She has held senior positions in international organizations. Currently, she wants to get closer to what really motivates her. Her dream is to set up an alternative school.

At the moment, however, she feels scattered, running around and suffering from her need to control everything. She doesn't really know what she wants professionally and finds it hard to accept her friends' judgments about her work. She feels lost and devalued. Her need to be perfect, to make a good impression, and to live up to the expectations of the people around her exhausts her.

Further, she suffers from facial blushing that can occur in any social situation and makes her feel ashamed. She's afraid of disappointing those around her and that they won't think she's up to the job. Her whole social life, both professional and personal, has been invaded, since adolescence, by this fear of blushing (erythrophobia), which has taken an enormous place in her life. Jeanne is also experiencing some tension in her relationship. As a hard-working person who always gives her all, she has little time for her partner, according to him. She also says she needs recognition from the people she admires in her work.

Growing up, Jeanne lived with her parents and her sister who was adopted at the age of 5 when Jeanne was 6. Their mother was depressed and attempted suicide by overdosing on medication when Jeanne was 13. Jeanne was the one who discovered her unconscious mother. Jeanne had gone out with friends and, fed up with her mother's solicitations, had not replied to her message asking Jeanne to come home and bake with her.

After this event, Jeanne assumed charge of everything in the family (budget, shopping, etc.), taking over from her mother who was not to be disturbed. She anticipated everything, including her sister's behavior, in order to make up for anything that might displease her mother. She complied with all her mother's demands, which were strict, unpredictable, and contradictory: show a good image of the family, don't talk at the table but talk anyway but not about everything, don't make noise, adopt certain lies in front of guests, and more. If the mother's demands were not met, she'd become emotionally overwhelmed (screaming, crying, humiliated) and shut herself in her room for days on end in a depressive mode. She would also sometimes leave the house. Jeanne would try to find her and beg her to come back. Her father, on the other hand, was loving but self-effacing. He would stand by and watch these situations and fall apart when his wife left. Jeanne tried to support him.

Jeanne also made it her mission to protect her sister, both at school when she was teased and at home, by hiding her mother's suicide attempt from her. She felt that her sister was fragile because of her difficult life (abandonment, adoption) and that it was up to Jeanne to help her. Jeanne therefore learned from childhood to control her emotions, needs, behaviors, and thoughts, as well as those of others. The image she presents to others became her main preoccupation.

At the age of 18, Jeanne left to study in another city. She experienced this move as a relief, freed from the burden of taking care of the family and controlling her mother's emotional reactions. However, her learned hyper-control carried through her studies and into her adult life.

Blushing Hell

The blushing began in junior high school and became more pronounced during her postgraduate studies. It occurred when speaking in class or in informal discussions and was often accompanied by humiliation on the part of adults. The high demands of her studies, particularly in terms of oral performance, exacerbated the situation. On several occasions, Jeanne was humiliated by a teacher but also mocked and scorned by other students. When she entered working life, the shame of blushing and the fear of not measuring up became even more pronounced. She was rubbing shoulders with people in high positions whom she considered to be brilliant, which raised her standards even higher. She tried to compensate by working at a frantic pace. Currently, blushing is the biggest problem in her life, both professionally and personally.

Jeanne attended cognitive behavior therapy (CBT) sessions on two occasions: during her studies and a few months before meeting me, her energy psychology practitioner. She also took part in group therapy. In addition, she consulted a dermatologist, who found nothing pathological about her blushing. She then considered the possibility of a surgical operation (sympathectomy: cutting or clamping a section of the sympathetic nervous system chain) that reduces physiological responses to strong emotions, but decided against it because of the risks involved (i.e., compensatory hyper-sweating, dry hands, slight drooping of the eyelid). She has always refused to take medication.

Jeanne's anxiety, blushing, erythrophobia, shame, avoidance, and fear of negative judgment by others led her therapist to hypothesize a social phobia. Jeanne has an intense fear that others will see her blushing in exposure situations (symptom of her anxiety) and judge her negatively (weak, emotional), so social situations almost always provoke anxiety in her. She doesn't avoid exposure situations in the professional and personal spheres but experiences them with great anxiety and shame.

Jeanne was developing great anxiety about her upcoming wedding. She was afraid of looking red in the photos and had been ever since she decided to get married (more than a year before the date). She thought about it almost every day and the fear was intense, disproportionate to the real threat. She'd had this anxiety, this fear of not being up to par in social situations, since middle school, so the symptoms had persisted for over six months (criterion for a diagnosis of social anxiety). Jeanne reported that this anxiety linked to blushing had altered her quality of life enormously, that it had been taking up all her space for years, and she felt great distress when she talked about it. She was not taking any substance that might trigger this anxiety and had no other medical condition. Her fear was not limited to performance situations, as it could be triggered in any social situation, such as an evening out with friends or a surprise from her partner.

According to the *Diagnostic and Statistical Manual of Mental Disorders, 5th Edition* (DSM-V; APA, 2016), these elements correspond to an anxiety disorder: social anxiety (social phobia). All criteria were present in Jeanne's case. Cognitively, she feared the negative judgment of others and developed perfectionism and low self-esteem; temperamentally, she displayed a certain emotionality; and behaviorally, she engaged in avoidance behaviors (using makeup to hide the blushing; running away on various pretexts) that reinforced her fears. She was also excessively self-centered, focusing on the slightest bodily warning signal that could herald the onset of blushing.

Erythrophobia

The DSM-V classifies erythrophobia (intense fear of blushing) as one of the symptoms of social anxiety. Social anxiety affects between 3% and 13% of the population and often begins in adolescence (APA, 2016). If left untreated, it can develop into a chronic condition. Few studies have focused specifically on erythrophobia, so its statistical prevalence is not yet known.

Erythrophobia is a fairly common problem, however. It can be very disabling for individuals and has its own specific features. Indeed, research has shown that people with erythrophobia have specific profiles compared to other people with social anxiety: later age of onset, less comorbidity, lower behavioral and temperamental inhibition and higher self-esteem, but high levels of social anxiety and impairment. Also "the specificity of fear of blushing needs to be considered within the spectrum of social anxiety, and can be viewed either as a subtype of social anxiety disorder, or as a form of social anxiety disorder secondary to fear of blushing" (Pelissolo et al., 2012).

Furthermore, some research puts forward "the idea that the fear of blushing is part of a broad spectrum of social anxiety that encompasses not only bodily symptoms but also other sources of negative evaluation and rejection" (Drummond & Gatt, 2018). It is these negative evaluation and rejection patterns that form the basis of the fear of blushing. Indeed, beliefs based on feeling different from others, and the need to hide one's thoughts and feelings for fear of their judgment, will reinforce the fear of blushing. The study authors explain that these patterns stem directly from traumatic experiences (e.g., being humiliated or mocked for blushing) and/or educational practices (e.g., using shame as a means of discipline), noting that "[t]he resulting patterns could increase predictions about the costs of blushing and trigger a fear response" (Drummond & Gatt, 2018).

Erythrophobia would therefore have its origins in traumas based on shame and humiliation, whether through educational attitudes on the part of parents or through direct experiences of humiliation aimed at blushing.

Jeanne's anamnesis revealed that her maternal upbringing was based on shame and concern for appearance. It was all about showing a certain image (determined by her mother) of herself and her family, which forbade Jeanne to give free rein to her thoughts or emotions. Jeanne had to be irreproachable in appearance, on pain of emotional reprisals or humiliation. A pattern of rejection and emotional inhibition set in, inducing a need to be perfect. It was against this backdrop that blushing appeared, as an expression of repressed emotions and a lasting reminder of the belief that she was different from everyone else. The fear of blushing, and therefore of being rejected or socially disapproved of, became increasingly intense, and the humiliating experiences of blushing reinforced this pattern, culminating in the development of erythrophobia.

Given these elements, I deemed it appropriate that Jeanne's therapy should be based on deconstructing these dysfunctional beliefs and patterns by dealing with the traumas that gave rise to them, but therapy should also offer anxiety reduction techniques to be used independently.

Energy Psychology

Energy psychology is a set of techniques that combine cognitive exposure (e.g., a traumatic memory) with action on the human energy system (such as tapping acupressure points, touch, or intention) for the psychotherapeutic purpose of restoring optimal emotional, cognitive, behavioral, and physical functioning. It is particularly useful in treating anxiety, trauma, limiting beliefs, and phobias.

The origins of energy psychology lie in both non-Western concepts such as traditional Chinese medicine and Western therapeutic approaches to analyzing psychological functioning.

Although energy psychology is a relatively recent discipline, the scientific literature of the past 10 years has seen an increasing amount of research devoted to it. These studies show that energy psychology and, in particular, Clinical EFT, has produced convincing results in the treatment of trauma and the management of stress and anxiety. By 2013, 23 randomized controlled trials and 17 within-subjects studies already provided evidence for the effectiveness of these methods (Church, 2013). In 2022, a review of 56 controlled trials reinforced these findings (Church et al., 2022).

Emotional Freedom Techniques (EFT)

Part of energy psychology is based on the stimulation of acupressure points through techniques such as EFT. It was clinical psychologist Roger Callahan (1985) who first integrated the stimulation of acupuncture points into a psychotherapeutic approach through the development of Thought Field Therapy (TFT). One of Callahan's students, Gary Craig, created a simplified form of TFT, which he dubbed Emotional Freedom Techniques (EFT; Craig and Fowlie, 1995). The fundamental EFT protocol is described in either of two comprehensive treatment manuals (Church, 2018; Craig and Fowlie, 1995). There are numerous variations of EFT, but the manualized form, Clinical EFT, is the one used in the many clinical studies confirming its effectiveness.

The EFT protocol, called the Basic Recipe, involves tapping a series of acupressure points with the fingers while uttering a phrase of acceptance of the memory or trauma that you wish to treat, followed by reminder phrases that maintain attention on the problem.

A study of 36 volunteers with a fear of public speaking showed that after a 45-minute EFT session, participants significantly reduced their fear. Subjective self-report measures were taken before, during, and after the session. Significant reductions in anxiety, measured with the Subjective Units of Distress (or Discomfort; SUD) scale, were demonstrated 15 minutes after the start of the session, then at 30 and 45 minutes. The authors concluded: "EFT has been shown to be an effective and rapid technique for treating fear of public speaking" (Jones et al., 2011).

The effectiveness of EFT in reducing anxiety was confirmed by observing a drop in cortisol levels in 83 subjects after an EFT session. Thirty minutes after the session, a significant reduction in anxiety (–58.34%, $p < 0.05$) and a significant drop in cortisol levels (–24.39%; SE, 2.61) were observed, in contrast to those observed in the control groups. The authors note: "The decrease in cortisol levels in the EFT group reflected the observed improvement in psychological distress" (Church, Yount, & Brooks, 2012). The study was replicated in 2020 with 53 participants. A significant reduction in cortisol levels (–43.24%, $p < .05$) was observed in the EFT group, greater than in the original study. The researchers concluded: "EFT may be an efficient and effective brief treatment for reducing biological markers of stress" (Stapleton et al., 2020).

A meta-analysis on the effect of EFT on anxiety evaluated 14 studies meeting the quality criteria for randomized controlled trials defined by division 12 of the American Psychological Association (APA). These studies included people suffering from anxiety, phobias, or PTSD, as well as volunteers with lower anxiety thresholds and in the academic field. The results showed: "The overall effect size for EFT treatment was 1.23 (95% confidence interval [CI], 0.82–1.64; $p < 0.001$). This effect size is considered large and is likely to be clinically significant. The study sample (PTSD, specific phobia, or other) was found to be a significant moderator ($p = 0.049$)." The author of the meta-analysis concluded: "These data demonstrate that EFT therapy is associated with a significant treatment effect when patients are compared with baseline or compared with control conditions" (Clond, 2016).

EFT has also been validated by various research studies in the treatment of PTSD. One such study showed that, in a group of abused adolescents, a single EFT session resulted in the disappearance of PTSD symptoms (Church, Piña, et al., 2012). Results were assessed using the SUD scale and the Event Impact Scale (EIS), which measures two components of PTSD: intrusive memories and avoidance symptoms. When reevaluated 30 days later, no improvement was found in the control group (mean total EIS before = 32 SD ±4.82; mean total EIS after = 31 SD ±3.84). In contrast, the authors note, "Posttest results for all participants in the experimental group improved to the point where all were non-clinical on the total score, as well as on the intrusive and avoidant symptom subscales, and on the SUD (mean total SEI pre = 36 SD ±4.74, post = 3 SD ±2.60, $p < 0.001$)" (Church, Piña, et al., 2012).

A meta-analysis carried out in 2023 evaluated the results of six studies on the effect of EFT on PTSD. These studies were selected from the scientific literature because they presented a randomized controlled sample and EFT was used to treat the symptoms of trauma or PTSD (or were a review of these studies). The authors reported: "Study quality and effect size were evaluated and the results demonstrated that treatment with Clinical EFT, when compared to wait list, usual care, or no treatment controls, resulted in significant and large effect sizes, ranging from 1.38 to 2.51. When compared to active controls, effect sizes ranged from –0.15 to 0.79, producing treatment results similar to other evidence-based therapies" (Stapleton et al., 2023).

Memory Reconsolidation

In addition to eliminating trauma symptoms, some research has found that EFT also helps to reconsolidate memories and extinguish emotional signals. Feinstein (2010) reviewed eight studies on the effects of acupuncture point stimulation on PTSD. Tapping on acupuncture points (acupoints) is a primary component of EFT, thus its informal name, "tapping." Feinstein concluded from the study results: "(a) tapping on selected acupoints, (b) during imaginal exposure, (c) quickly and permanently reduces maladaptive fear responses to traumatic memories and related cues." The Clinical EFT protocol enables the brain to deconstruct certain ideas or beliefs emanating directly from traumas, sometimes very consolidated, and to bring out a new vision of the world, of oneself, or of others, replacing the old one.

This is memory reconsolidation, which is defined as the "process by which an outdated learning can be transformed while activated, forming new neural pathways that are then integrated into the memory system, replacing earlier representations" (Feinstein, 2018).

In this way, the neuronal pathways involved in symptoms are durably modified. This differs from extinction, in which new neuronal pathways are created while the old ones are still present, running the risk of the symptom recurring.

This reconsolidation of memories was observed in a study of four women with dental fear who underwent four sessions of EFT (Cartland, 2016). At the end of the treatment, the four women saw their dental fear and/or anxiety decrease significantly, and for three of them, the negative dental beliefs were also modified. In addition, the three subjects who responded to the follow-up questions reported that the results were maintained or even improved.

Clinical EFT has proven its effectiveness in the treatment of trauma and anxiety. Reconsolidating memories also enables the cognitive changes needed to modify beliefs and therefore the patterns and behaviors that arise from them.

In the treatment of erythrophobia, EFT can be applied to the traumas underlying patterns of rejection and emotional inhibition but also directly to the anxiety generated by blushing situations.

Further Analysis of Jeanne's Erythrophobia

To analyze Jeanne's problem behavior further, we explored a target situation: an evening out with friends. This is one of the typical social situations in which Jeanne's fear of blushing most often manifests itself.

Figure 1 illustrates Jeanne's reactions, emotions, thoughts, and behaviors in a problem situation. As illustrated by the arrows in the figure, this situation immediately provokes emotions of shame, sadness, anxiety, a feeling of worthlessness, and a physical sensation of heat. She then attributes a personal meaning to these emotions and sensations ("My partner will be ashamed of me," "I'll be rejected or denigrated," "I'll be thought a loser"), a meaning that immediately triggers cognitions such as "I don't measure up," "I'm ugly," and "I'm not like the others." These cognitions then take the form of images in which she sees herself all red and sees others pointing out her blush.

This cycle of personal meaning (cognitions and images) reinforces the sensations and emotions previously experienced, which in turn trigger the blushing symptom and related compensatory behaviors (Jeanne pretends to make a phone call so she can go out; she puts her hair over her face to hide her redness; she focuses her attention on bodily warning signals). The need for perfection, control, and concealment of her erythrophobia from those around her creates more and more suffering for Jeanne. It also provokes anticipation of future situations: "I'll blush, I'll look weak, emotional, not up to it." Thus when a situation arises again, the whole cycle is reactivated.

Table 1 presents the elements of Jeanne's anamnesis likely to provide information on the functioning of her erythrophobia. It shows us how the disorder developed and was maintained, exploring possible structural data (linked to failures of attachment figures), possible historical maintenance factors (in particular, high familial demands, humiliations suffered, and concealment of erythrophobia), initial triggers invoked (first blushes and humiliations), events precipitating the disorder (prestigious student and professional environment), other problems (preoccupation with perfection), and previous treatments (psychotherapies).

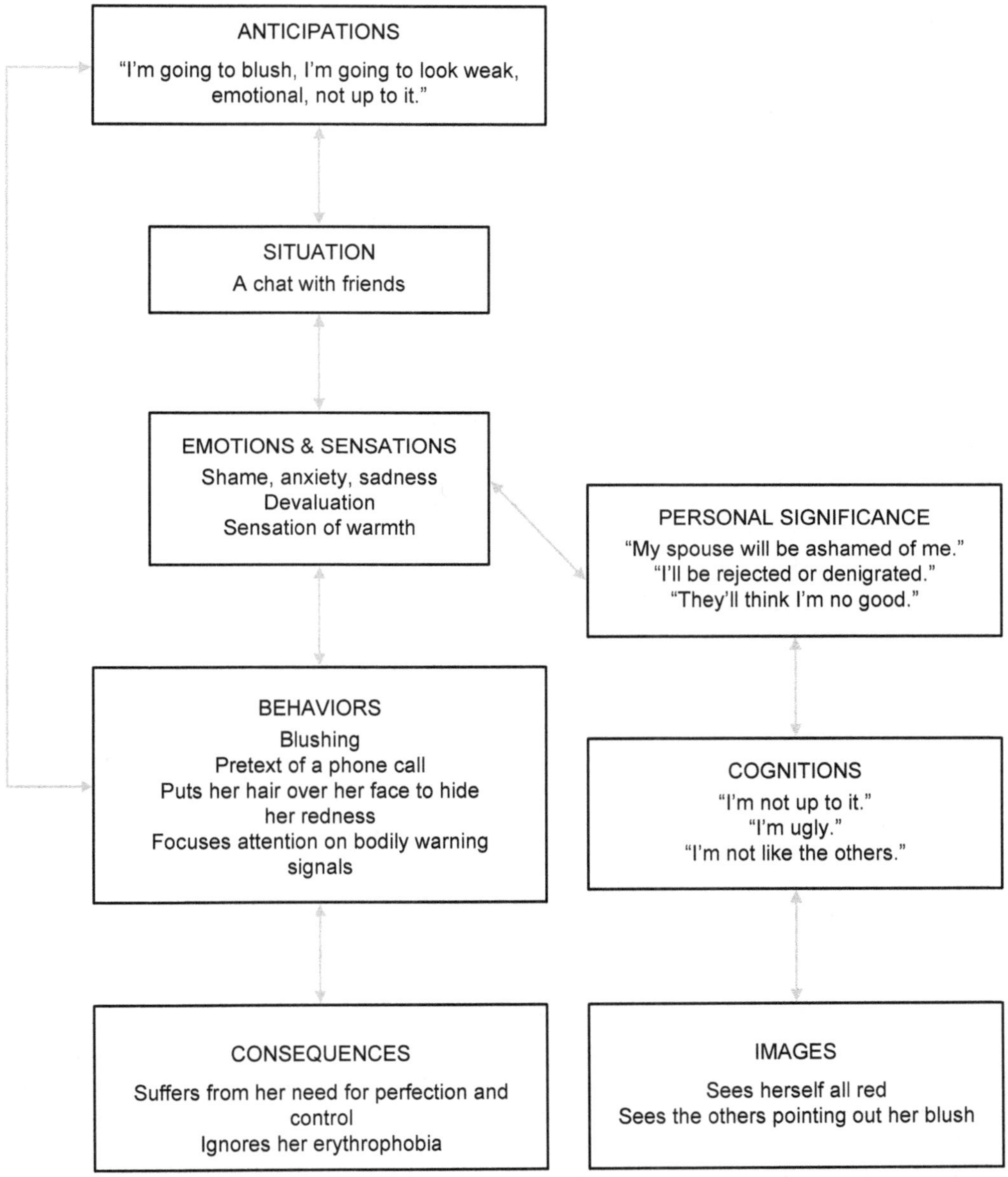

Figure 1. A synchronic functional analysis of an erythrophobic situation for Jeanne: a discussion between friends. The double arrows in the diagram illustrate that each component of the cycle triggers the next but also reinforces the previous one. The outer double arrow indicates that the whole cycle is reactivated by the aggravating factors.

Table 1. *Origin and Maintenance Factors*

Possible Structural Data

- Attachment figures: depressive mother and self-effacing father
- Childhood and adolescence marked by shame and preoccupation with appearances
- Taking charge of the family and anticipating conflicts to compensate for her mother's failings

Possible Historical Maintenance Factors

- Maternal instructions to give others a good image of the family and to respect its requirements in terms of rules of life
- Protection of her sister, mocked at school
- Humiliation during higher education
- Has always hidden erythrophobia

Initial Triggers Invoked

- Blushing as early as middle school, blushing in class or in social situations
- When speaking in class during school, humiliation by teachers and students
- Feeling different from others

Precipitating Events

- Higher education at a Grande École (elite French institution of higher education) where she did not have the same sociocultural background as the other students
- Prestigious, demanding socio-professional environment

Other Problems

- Shame of not being perfect
- Feeling of not measuring up

Previous Treatments

- No drug treatment
- Saw two CBT psychologists and did group therapy

Note: CBT = cognitive behavior therapy.

Erythrophobia Roots in Childhood

Jeanne's childhood was marked by her mother's strict injunctions: to hide her emotions, to speak only in such a way as to show a good family image, and not to behave "noisily." If these subjective rules were not respected, her mother's emotions would boil over and she could withdraw for days at a time. Jeanne therefore learned to comply with these demands. In this way, she tried to avoid the humiliation, rejection, anger, and guilt that followed. She also took charge of the whole family and tried to control her sister's behavior and emotions in order to keep the family together and compensate for her father's self-effacing attitude. This impossible role forced her to suppress her emotions, thoughts, and needs and control everything, leading her to feel different from others and not good enough.

When the blushes appeared in adolescence, out of emotion (repressed) or heat or cold, Jeanne saw them as a sign of emotionality and weakness likely to be judged negatively by others (since she had learned she had to be perfect). She was afraid of being rejected (as she had learned from her mother's behavior toward her). As a result, she focused on her blushing and tried to control it, without succeeding, of course. These failures generated anxiety, anger, and shame, emotions that in turn provoked blushing. She thus entered a state of permanent vigilance, on the lookout for any bodily sensation that might alert her to the slightest hint of blushing, which in turn only aggravated the blushing. Gradually, all social situations became a source of anxiety. The vicious circle of erythrophobia was in place. Then the humiliations and remarks she suffered when speaking in class or directed at her blushing, and later the high demands of the professional environments in which she was involved, amplified and reinforced her symptom.

After hearing this analysis during the third session, Jeanne was moved. "It's the first time I've seen things from this angle," she said, "and I'm aware of the link with what I experienced as a child." At the time, however, she didn't see the psychological violence she had suffered as trauma and remained concerned about protecting her parents.

Methodology

The therapeutic plan for Jeanne was threefold. First, she would learn to manage her anxiety independently using Clinical EFT (the manualized version of EFT; Church, 2018). Using digital stimulation (tapping) on acupuncture points (acupoints) on the head, face, torso, and hands, EFT calms the brain structures involved in detecting fear and thus rapidly alleviates anxiety and stress. The aim here is to install resources that should help reduce anticipatory anxiety and form an initial breach in the emotional loop. Indeed, knowing that she would now have the means to manage her emotions of anxiety and shame when they arose, Jeanne would likely develop less fear of the onset of blushing. This step would also strengthen the therapeutic alliance, as Jeanne would experience how to soothe and accept her suffering, with empathy. Along with these additional resources, Jeanne already benefited from a supportive environment. She was surrounded by friends, her partner was present, and she had many interesting professional encounters. At this point in the therapy, she would have all the resources she needed to carry out the work of the second stage.

The second part of the work used Energetic Memory Reconsolidation Therapy. This consists of emotionally deactivating the traumas at the root of beliefs with a reparenting protocol using EFT, which involves accompanying the person into their past, enabling them to help the child they were in certain difficult situations they experienced, in order to "purge" them of their traumatic charge. "[T]he person being supported then becomes an actress in a play, invited by the director-therapist to take to the stage to comfort and emotionally liberate her younger double, who carries the trauma and has remained frozen in time" (Gurret, 2021). The new scene is then integrated into her energy system, leading to memory reconsolidation. By eliminating the emotional charge of the memory and integrating a new scene, this technique enables new conclusions to be drawn from what has been experienced, thus modifying the limiting beliefs generated. Replacing these old limiting beliefs with new, positive ones enables the dysfunctional patterns (of rejection, for example) to be abandoned, thus creating a new breach in the emotional loop of erythrophobia.

The third stage of therapy consisted of psycho-education, explaining to Jeanne, as often as necessary as the sessions progressed, the role of past trauma in her current symptoms. As Jeanne was always concerned not to blame her parents (which prevented her from realizing the impact of their attitudes on her psyche), she gradually came to realize, through this psycho-education approach, that therapy does not put her parents on trial, but rather deals with events that are still emotionally charged today and which were of her parents' making (however unintentional). This would enable her to see more clearly the links between her current beliefs and what she learned through her upbringing, and thus be able to question her beliefs. The psycho-education also reiterated the importance of breaking the blushing reinforcement loop and the need to accept any blushing that might occur as part of being human. The aim was to change Jeanne's vision of blushing, until she understood that the primary aim of therapy is not to eliminate blushing, but to eliminate fear, as in any phobia. The blushing would then diminish (or disappear) on its own. Jeanne immediately accepted this therapeutic plan, which made sense to her.

Thorough Therapy

A total of 15 therapy sessions were carried out. The first three sessions were devoted to anamnesis, goal setting, developing the therapeutic plan, and consolidating the alliance. The next two sessions were, as planned, devoted to learning Clinical EFT. The remaining ten sessions focused on emotionally deactivating the memories that had contributed to the rejection and inhibition pattern. The energy and emotional techniques used enabled me to identify the events to be treated while respecting Jeanne's process.

Two of the sessions took place outside this framework, however. In my commitment to follow Jeanne's progress and not impose a fixed plan on her, which would not respect her and would therefore be counterproductive, I chose to deal with Jeanne's present concerns as they arose. Thus one session was devoted to a relationship problem she was encountering at work and another session to a family problem with which Jeanne was having difficulty coping. These sessions appeared to be essential, first to calm Jeanne at the time and enable her to overcome her difficulties, but also because these emotional states would not have afforded her the necessary resources to progress in the ongoing work.

Finally, some sessions left plenty of room for psycho-education, particularly when Jeanne tended to minimize the effects of her upbringing on her current beliefs and behaviors. I explained the notion of childhood trauma, attachment, and psycho-corporal repercussions. I paid particular attention to the right moments for distilling this information, that is, when Jeanne was in a position to integrate it.

For example, I wasn't able to tackle the notion of accepting blushing until the 10th session, as Jeanne was initially too focused on eliminating her blushing as the only solution to the problem. As a result, I brought up the subject of acceptance by drawing a parallel with spider phobia, in which the aim of therapy is not to eliminate the spiders, but rather the fear. The same applies to erythrophobia: The aim is not to eliminate the blushing, but to eliminate the fear. I couldn't have explained this to her at the start of therapy, at the risk, at best, of her not integrating it, at worst, of losing the alliance and her stopping therapy. My guiding principle has therefore always been to respect the client's progress, to assess the state of her resources at the start of each session, to move forward at her own pace, without imposing a pre-established plan that she wouldn't accept. EFT, as a client-centered method, fits completely into this framework. A client-centered focus allows the client to control the flow of the session and take charge of their own healing, empowers the client rather than creating dependence on the practitioner, and promotes self-generated solutions that are congruent with the client (Church, 2018).

Clinical EFT

During the presentation of the therapeutic plan, we had agreed that Jeanne would learn Clinical EFT to manage her anxiety in stressful or triggering situations. Thus, in the fourth session, I suggested that she learn this technique by experimenting with a relatively recent event of erythrophobia. I chose not to treat an older and/or more traumatic event directly, as I didn't yet know how Jeanne reacts when remembering distressing events: What is her window of tolerance,[1] does she dissociate, and what is the risk of emotional overreaction? This first application of Clinical EFT would enable me to assess her resources and reactions and to envisage ways of working in subsequent sessions.

I explained to her how Clinical EFT works: "It involves stimulating energy meridian entry or exit points with the fingertips, while focusing on a negative emotion linked to a specific traumatic event. This stimulation will activate your parasympathetic system, your body's calming response. As the points are gradually stimulated, this calming response will take over, eliminating the negative emotion that prevailed until then. The emotional charge will have completely disappeared and you'll be able to see things differently."

I suggested that she experiment on her own and find an event to process that related to her problem. She agreed and chose the following event: A professor humiliated her in front of the other students during an oral exam in her graduate studies.

The following are two of Jeanne's sessions that demonstrate the use of energy psychology. The memory Jeanne chose regarding the professor is the one we worked on in Session Example 1.

Session Example 1: Clinical EFT

Annick the therapist (T): "How do you feel about going to work on this memory?"

Jeanne (J): "I'm fine. I don't feel anything in particular."

As Jeanne didn't seem to have any problems with the memory, I decided to apply Clinical EFT's Basic Recipe, the standard protocol. (In the midst of a trauma reaction, other EFT techniques are needed to circumvent retraumatization.)

T: "Focus on the most emotionally intense moment in the scene for you right now... What is that moment, that image? What do you see?"

J: "This is the moment when I can't speak, I don't know the answer, it's like a blank. The teacher tells me that he doesn't accept this in his class, that I'm provoking him, and that I don't belong in

[1] The concept of the tolerance window is central to the work of Daniel Siegel, Pat Ogden, and Kekuni Minton, and represents the range of emotional intensity that each of us is capable of feeling. Individuals can therefore feel safe, learn, and enjoy life within this range, or window. They can also talk about and free themselves from traumas and difficult experiences when they remain within this window. This is an important point of focus for every practitioner.

this school. He belittles me in front of the whole class. The students smile and look at each other."

T: "What are you feeling right now?"

J: "Shame."

T: "On a scale of 0 to 10, what would that shame be?"

J: "9."

T: "This shame, where do you feel it in your body?"

J: "In my solar plexus."

T: "What do you tell yourself about yourself, right now, seeing this image?"

J: "I tell myself I don't belong in this school, I'm useless, I'm weak."

T: "We're going to do a round of EFT. You tap on the points on you at the same time as I do on me, while repeating what I say."

I then tapped on the side of the hand point while uttering the following sentences and Jeanne did the same.

Side of the hand: "Even if I feel this shame because this teacher humiliated me in front of the whole class, I love and accept myself as I am. Even if I feel this shame in my solar plexus because this teacher humiliated me and accused me of provoking him, I love and accept myself as I am. Even if I feel this shame at a 9 because that teacher humiliated me, just because I didn't have the answer, I love and accept myself as I am."

I then tapped all the points of the EFT round, with Jeanne doing the same.

Top of head (TH): All the shame I feel.

Beginning of the eyebrow (EB): He humiliated me.

Side of the eye (SE): He told me I didn't belong in this school.

Under the eye (UE): He said I was provoking him.

Under the nose (UN): All this shame in my solar plexus.

Chin (Ch): Students look at each other and smile.

Collarbones (CB): I can't speak.

Under the arm (UA): I can't defend myself.

Under the breasts/nipples (UN): The whole class looking at me.

Corner of the nail of the thumb (Th): This shame at 9 in my plexus.

Corner of index finger nail (IN): All the shame I feel.

Middle finger (MF): This teacher who's always picking on me.

Little finger (LF): Students who smile.

Gamut point (GP): The teacher who humiliates me.

At the end of the EFT round, the SUD level had dropped to 5. Jeanne still felt shame in her solar plexus. Above all, she saw the students whispering to each other and the teacher unmoving and tall in front of her. Jeanne and I did a second EFT round, starting with the sentence: "Even though I still feel ashamed when I see the students whispering to each other and the tall, unmoving teacher in front of me, I love and accept myself as I am."

At the end of the round, Jeanne's SUD score was at 0. She was now angry with the teacher, feeling the anger in her belly at SUD 6. We did an EFT round, starting with the sentence: "Even though I'm angry with this teacher because he humiliated me in front of everyone, just because I didn't have the answer, and took advantage of my position as a student who couldn't defend herself, I love and accept myself as I am."

At the end of the round, the SUD rating was at 0. Jeanne now felt sadness at 6 in her chest. She was sad because she couldn't defend herself and was alone against this teacher. Jeanne and I did two rounds of EFT, starting with the sentence: "Even though I have this sadness in my chest because I was all alone with this teacher, unable to defend myself, I love and accept myself as I am." The SUD level went down to 4 and then 0.

At this stage, no negative emotional traces remained.

T: "What do you tell yourself when you think back to that scene now?"

J: "I tell myself that this teacher was really ridiculous, that he had a problem."

T: "How do you feel now?"

J: "I feel tired, drained."

Jeanne's cognition had changed and the emotional charge had disappeared. Memory reconsolidation had taken place. At the beginning of the session, Jeanne felt ashamed and told herself that she didn't belong in this school, that she was weak and useless. At the end of the EFT session, Jeanne no longer felt shame or any other embarrassing emotion when recalling this memory and had a totally different vision of it: She told herself it was the teacher who had a problem, he was really ridiculous, and it was not her. When the client reports SUD 0 and it holds at 0 when the client resummons that memory, the work of memory reconsolidation is complete (Church, 2015).

Jeanne then told me that a memory came back to her during the rounds: She was a teenager and had been wrongly accused of stealing from a store. We dealt with this memory in the next session.

I explained to Jeanne that she could use EFT on a daily basis to deal with her emotions when she felt overwhelmed. This would also have the effect of deconditioning the anxiety reflexes she had developed in social situations. I provided her with a diagram showing the location of the acupressure points used in EFT, along with brief instructions so she could carry out the protocol on her own.

Jeanne has embraced EFT because she has experienced its power over her emotions. She agreed to continue working with me and to use EFT independently. In my opinion, this session achieved its objectives: to teach Jeanne a technique that would make her autonomous, to encourage her acceptance of it by measuring its effects on her, and to strengthen the therapeutic alliance. It also enabled her to deal with a traumatic event linked to her erythrophobia and thus begin to deconstruct the underlying patterns.

Session Example 2: Memory Reconsolidation

At the 11th session, as at the beginning of every session, I reviewed the situation with Jeanne regarding erythrophobia:

- Number of erythrophobia situations experienced this week: 3
- Anxiety about blushing: 5/10

I also made sure she was still willing to work on her erythrophobia and that the conditions in which it manifests had not changed. The phobia manifests when she's with people and doesn't feel up to it (friends or professionals). She feels ashamed, which is amplified if someone points out that she's red (blushing).

In this session, we continued to work on her negative beliefs, processing a network of events that contributed to their construction. I asked her to choose a memory, a moment when she blushed and felt this shame in a very intense way. She recalled a scene from her student days. In a classroom, the tables were arranged in a U-shape and everyone had to state the name of the radio station they were listening to. Listening to France Inter or France Culture was what was valued at this Grande École. As her father was used to listening to another general-interest radio station and so was she, Jeanne thought she could say she listened to this one. But all the students whispered among themselves and scorned this choice. Jeanne blushed and felt ashamed.

I suggested that she treat this event with Energetic Memory Reconsolidation Therapy. This technique is based on the trace we retain in our unconscious of traumatic events experienced in our past. Karl Dawson, the founder of one of these methods, Matrix Reimprinting, called these memories "echoes," or "Energetic Consciousness Holograms." In fact, they are the parts of ourselves that are often dissociated and inaccessible to our consciousness, stuck in a state of powerlessness in our energy field, profoundly alone and isolated, unable to act effectively.

In this session, the aim was to go back to earlier events that might be at the root of Jeanne's erroneous beliefs. The advantage of this process is that it short-circuits the mind, giving access to linked memories that might not otherwise have arisen. The therapist asks the client to project the memory scene onto an imaginary screen we call the matrix. She then invites the client to enter the scene in her adult form, with all her present resources, to help the younger version of herself digest the traumatic or difficult event.

As this protocol is a tool that relies on dissociation, Jeanne, who tends to dissociate, quickly made it her own. She entered the matrix, saw the scene with herself in the classroom, just after speaking. I checked that she was dissociating by asking her what the younger version of herself was wearing. I then asked her to introduce herself to her "echo" and ask its permission to help her. When her younger self agreed, we proceeded.

T: "Ask your echo how she feels."

J: "Shame and sadness."

T: "Where is it in her body and how does it feel? Ask her."

J: "It's in her chest. Like a weight."

T: "That weight of shame and sadness, that sensation in her body, ask her when she felt it the very first time."

J: "... When she was 12 or 13, she was doing theater and had to draw lots to do an improvisation with a boy, who impressed her. She still feels ashamed. She's afraid of not knowing what to say, of not being funny."

Again, we moved from echo to echo, starting with the emotion of shame and the bodily sensation of the second echo, until we arrived at a new memory. She was in grade 6. While answering a question in class, she blushed and felt ashamed. No other scene presented itself to the echo.

We will therefore deal with the three memories, starting with the last to appear: the scene in grade 6.

Note: This method is a variant of EFT. The client sits with her eyes closed. She imagines she is stimulating the EFT points directly on her younger self. The therapist performs the stimulations directly on the client, with her prior consent. The therapist suggests phrases to the client, who repeats them if she agrees, while she lets the practitioner stimulate her own points. This is the method used in Matrix Reimprinting.

I stimulated the EFT points on Jeanne's fingers while she continued to talk to her younger self.

T: "Ask your echo how she feels."

J: "She feels shame. In her chest. She sees the eyes on her, she's afraid of making a mistake."

The SUD level was at 8. We performed an EFT round in imagination on the echo, and in reality on Jeanne, to reduce the shame.

Side of the hand: "Even if you have this shame in your chest because you're speaking in front of the class, and all the students are looking at you and you're afraid of making a mistake, you're a wonderful girl and I'm here for you."

TH: That shame in your chest.

EB: All the students are looking at you.

SE: You're afraid of making a mistake.

UE: All that shame in your chest.

UN: You're blushing.

Ch: All those eyes on you.

CB: You're afraid of making a mistake.

The SUD rating went down to 3. As a second round of EFT on the echo, we started with: "Even if you feel shame in your chest because the students are looking at you and you're blushing, you're a wonderful girl and I'm here for you." After that, the SUD level dropped to 0—no more negative emotions.

T: "What did your echo believe at that moment, about herself, others, or the world?"

J: "How ridiculous she was."

T: "Tell your echo that she can transform this scene so she has everything she needed at that moment to feel really good."

Jeanne transformed the scene by bringing in her grandmother as a resource to support her.

T: "How does the echo feel now?"

J: "Soothed.

T: "What color would this soothed feeling be?"

J: "Green."

T: "And what texture would it have?"

J: "Light, like a veil."

We proceeded to reimprint these resources energetically in order to create new neural circuits. To do this, I asked Jeanne to place her hand on her heart and, while tapping on the 9 Gamut point, project the sensation of the light, green soothing like a veil into her head, her neurons, her body, her cells, and then her heart, then amplify this sensation and send it out into her entire energy field around her and into the whole Universe. The procedure is the same for all the following energetic reimprints.

Using this procedure, we then made an energetic reimprint of the memory of the theater improvisation, when she was 12–13 years old. In this way, we retraced the chain of events that formed the belief of being ridiculous. Jeanne visualized the scene: She saw her echo as she drew the improvisation subjects. We performed three rounds of EFT on the echo, which was experiencing panic at 9/10. A psychological reversal prevented her from letting go of this panic. I decided simply to ask this part to let us work. If that was not enough, we would treat the reversal by massaging the Sore Spot (located on either side of the chest about two inches from the sternum and three inches below the collarbone; rubbing it helps alleviate anxiety).

Psychological Reversal

The concept of psychological reversal is specific to the field of energy therapies and signifies that "when your energies are blocked or reversed, you develop symptoms" (Church, 2018). It is a polarity inversion in the body that impedes the free flow of energy, as in a battery that has been plugged in backward. In EFT, we may suspect psychological reversals when the treatment of a problem is not progressing. The person has a deep-seated desire to change a behavior or free themselves from a problem, but an unconscious block prevents them from doing so. This is often the case with symptoms that resist various therapies (addictions and chronic pain in particular). By using the acceptance phrase in the protocol, EFT removes these psychological reversals.

I asked Jeanne if she could isolate the part of her that was panicking and ask that part to step aside to let us work. She could stand by and intervene if things didn't work out. The part agreed. The echo now felt sadness at 5. We did two rounds of EFT and the sadness disappeared. There were no more negative emotions: "She feels good and she knows she can be funny." Her belief was the same as before: She thought she was being ridiculous. Jeanne then transformed the scene: She took herself, an adult, as a resource, and little Jeanne did her improv and was funny. Jeanne now felt pride, reporting it as a yellow color with a metallic texture. We proceeded to the energetic reimprint of this new resource.

Finally, we reimprinted the last scene: her choice of radio during her studies. But when I asked her how the echo felt, she replied, "The echo feels good, it's slipping over her." The work we did on the other two scenes had deactivated the emotional charge of this one, confirming that we were indeed dealing with emotionally connected scenes that contributed to the creation of the belief of being ridiculous.

We then came to the transformation of the scene. It once again took the adult Jeanne as a resource, and the echo asserted herself and confidently asked the students what was wrong with listening to this radio station. Jeanne again felt pride with a yellow color and metallic texture. We proceeded to the energy reimprint of this new resource. I could see the pride on her face and the strength it gave her. It was moving. Jeanne emerged from the matrix. She reported feeling soothed and seeing the scene "from afar."

I pointed out that her blushing, avoidance behaviors, shame, anxiety, sadness, and all the cognitions and images that stem from them were based on the belief "I'm ridiculous." She was astonished by this and remembered that, as a child, she had loved performing and acting, being funny. She didn't remember when the belief came to stop her.

This work enabled us to unwind the thread of the belief that she was being ridiculous. First, we eliminated the emotional charge linked to the events, which had the effect of enabling her to adopt a different view of things (e.g., she now knows she can be funny). Second, by transforming the scenes and reimprinting them energetically, Jeanne was able to recover the resources she needed for self-assertion, self-confidence, and public exposure. These resources are now in her field.

This session represented a turning point in the therapy. The following week, Jeanne realized she hadn't blushed in two situations that would have prompted it before. At the time, she was astonished but then thought no more about it, carrying on with her work. She had forgotten about her erythrophobia.

Discussion

In previous sessions, we had worked with the same process, but on different memories linked to Jeanne's upbringing, her mother's suicide attempt, and her radical reactions. The Session Example 2 was therefore part of a continuum and did not, on its own, have an effect on Jeanne's erythrophobia. It was the whole series of sessions that gradually helped to deconstruct beliefs and patterns.

The rest of the therapy continued in the same vein. The last session, before Jeanne's wedding, consisted of a sequence of EFT on anxiety and all the negative emotions that arose in connection with her wedding day. We then carried out an energy reimprint of the future, to give her the maximum resources to live this day.

Following her wedding, Jeanne stopped the therapy. She'd had no problem with blushing on her wedding day and sent me a photo in which, indeed, no redness is perceptible.

As noted, numerous studies have demonstrated the effectiveness of EFT in the treatment of phobias and anxiety (Church et al., 2022). The results obtained with Jeanne corroborate these research results: reduction of fear and anxiety linked to the object of the phobia (blushing, in Jeanne's case), and positively modified cognitions.

EFT has a double advantage. On the one hand, it effectively advances therapy by treating traumas and painful memories in depth and in a lasting way, thanks to the reconsolidation of memories it enables. EFT is a gentle method that, when accompanied by a therapist, enables safe work on traumas, treating problems at their roots. On the other hand, it gives people a tool for working independently and calming down in problematic exposure situations in their daily lives. It's a simple method that can be learned quickly. The aim of therapy is to give the person the means to be free and autonomous, not to create dependency on the therapist.

The main problem I encountered was Jeanne's lack of work between sessions. Despite her initial commitment, she rarely used EFT independently in situations of anxiety or erythrophobia. Several reminders from me were not enough to change her behavior. Perhaps she had secondary benefits from keeping some of the erythrophobia, which I was unable to identify.

On the other hand, although EFT is a very effective technique, it is not in itself a sufficient basis for therapy. The therapeutic alliance is the main driving force. It was easily established with Jeanne: She said she trusted me completely, told me things she'd never told anyone before, and immediately adhered to the therapeutic plan. While this situation was comfortable from the outset, I had to be careful to maintain it throughout the therapy. At various points, I repositioned the framework so she would work between sessions and not wait for a miracle solution from me. I also reminded her of her responsibility to get better, at the risk of alienating her and losing the alliance. I then understood that the therapist is constantly on a knife edge, balancing between the necessary progress of the therapy, and therefore the client's confrontation with certain realities, and the risk of losing the therapeutic alliance, which would signal the failure of the therapy. This requires listening to the person beyond their words, respecting their rhythm, and understanding and accepting the way they function. But it also requires the therapist to deal with her own biases, so as to be able to adapt her posture and choose the right words, tone, and moments to intervene.

Conclusion

In this case study, we have been able to see how Clinical EFT and Energetic Memory Reconsolidation Therapy can be used as part of a therapeutic process to alleviate the symptoms of a young woman suffering from social anxiety following a tumultuous start in life.

This 15-session therapy, based on energy techniques, made it possible to treat her social anxiety and erythrophobia by targeting their sources. The emotional release of traumatic memories and the installation of new resources enabled the reconsolidation of memories and the cognitive changes necessary for a new vision of herself, others, and the world.

This case study demonstrates that energy techniques have a place in psychotherapy and increase its effectiveness. These techniques enabled me to work in depth, targeting the life events that had led Jeanne to develop limiting beliefs ("I'm ridiculous, I'm useless, I'm weak, I must be perfect"), which in turn generated the corresponding behaviors (erythrophobia, avoidance, attempts to control everything). Thanks to the contribution of energy techniques, the therapy was able to act on the emotional impact of traumatic memories, enabling Jeanne to deconstruct her limiting beliefs gradually and then abandon inappropriate behaviors.

References

American Psychiatric Association (APA). (2016). *Mini DSM-5 diagnostic criteria*. Elsevier Masson.

Cartland, A. M. (2016). Emotional Freedom Techniques (EFT) remediates dental fear: A case series. *Energy Psychology: Theory, Research, and Treatment, 8*(2), 42–66. doi:10.9769/EPJ.2016.8.2.AC

Church, D. (2013). Clinical EFT as an evidence-based practice for the treatment of psychological and physiological conditions. *Psychology, 4*(8), 645–654. doi:10.4236/psych.2013.48092

Church, D. (2015). *Psychological trauma: Treating its roots in brain, body, and memory to heal*. Energy Psychology Press.

Church, D. (2018). *The EFT manual* (4th ed.). Energy Psychology Press.

Church, D., Piña, O., Reategui, C. & Brooks, A. (2012). Single-session reduction of the intensity of traumatic memories in abused adolescents after EFT: a randomized controlled pilot study. *Traumatology, 18*(3), 73–79. doi:10.1177/1534765611426788

Church, D., Stapleton, P., Vasudevan, A., & O'Keefe, T. (2022). Clinical EFT as an evidence-based practice for the treatment of psychological and physiological conditions: A systematic review. *Frontiers in Psychology, 13*, 951451. doi:10.3389/fpsyg.2022.951451

Church, D., Yount, G. & Brooks, A. (2012). The effect of Emotional Freedom Techniques on stress biochemistry: A randomized controlled trial. *Journal of Nervous and Mental Disease, 200*(10), 891–896. doi:10.1097/NMD.0b013e31826b9fc1

Clond, M. (2016). Emotional Freedom Techniques for anxiety: A systematic review with meta-analysis. *Journal of Nervous and Mental Disease, 204*(5), 388–395. doi:10.1097/NMD.0000000000000483

Drummond, P. & Gatt, J. (2018). Early maladaptive schemas in people with a fear of blushing. *Clinical Psychologist, 22*(2), 203–210. doi:10.1111/cp.12114

Feinstein, D. (2010). Rapid treatment of PTSD: Why psychological exposure with acupoint tapping may be effective. *Psychotherapy: Theory, Research, Practice, Training, 47*(3), 385–402. doi:10.1037/a0021171

Feinstein, D. (2018). Energy psychology: Efficacy, speed, mechanisms. *Explore: The Journal of Science and Healing, 15*(5), 340–351. doi:10.1016/j.explore.2018.11.003

Gurret, J. M. (2021, 24 novembre). *De l'héritabilité épigénétique à la reconsolidation des mémoires* [Conférence]. *Congrès sur le Trauma et l'attachement*. Retrieved from https://ifpec.org/heritabilite-epigenetique-reconsolidation-des-memoires/

Jones, S., Thornton, J. & Andrews, H. (2011). Efficacy of Emotional Freedom Techniques (EFT) in reducing public speaking anxiety: A randomized controlled trial. *Energy Psychology: Theory, Research, and Treatment, 3*(1), 19–32. doi:10.9769.EPJ.2011.3.1.SJ

Laederach-Hofmann, K., Mussgay, L., Büchel, B., Widler, P., & Rüddel, H. (2002). Patients with erythrophobia (fear of blushing) show abnormal autonomic regulation in mental stress conditions. *Psychosomatic Medicine, 64*(2), 358–365. doi:10.1097/00006842-200203000-00022

Pelissolo, A., Moukheiber, A., Lobjoie, C., Valla, J. & Lambrey, S. (2012). Is there a place for fear of blushing in social anxiety spectrum? *Depression and Anxiety, 29*(1), 62–70. doi:10.1002/da.20851

Stapleton, P., Crighton, G., Sabot, D., & O'Neill, H. M. (2020, March 12). Reexamining the effect of emotional freedom techniques on stress biochemistry: A randomized controlled trial. *Psychological Trauma: Theory, Research, Practice, and Policy, 12*(8), 869–877. doi:10.1037/tra0000563

Stapleton, P., Kip, K., Church, D., Toussaint, L., Footman, J., Ballantyne, P., & O'Keefe, T. (2023). Emotional freedom techniques for treating post traumatic stress disorder: An updated systematic review and meta-analysis. *Frontiers in Psychology, 14*, 1195286. doi:10.3389/fpsyg.2023.1195286

If you would like to write book reviews for Energy Psychology *journal, we'd love to hear from you. Get inspiring books for free! Contact Stephanie Marohn at angel@stephaniemarohn.com*

Tapping: Self-Healing with the Transformative Power of Energy Psychology

David Feinstein, PhD, and Donna Eden

Sounds True, 2024
Softcover, 432 pages
$25.99
ISBN: 978-1683649960

Reviewed by Dawson Church

Imagine having a solution to worry, stress, anxiety, and negative thinking at your fingertips. That's the promise of energy psychology, the best-known format of which is Emotional Freedom Techniques, or EFT. It is colloquially referred to as "tapping" because it uses fingertip tapping on acupuncture points to release troubling emotions.

Renowned psychologist David Feinstein and his wife, energy medicine pioneer Donna Eden, have teamed up to write an authoritative new guide called *Tapping: Self-Healing with the Transformative Power of Energy Psychology.*

More than 170 scientific studies show that tapping is effective for a wide variety of physical and psychological issues. When we tap on acupoints, our levels of fear, anger, loneliness, sadness, and similar emotions often drop quickly and dramatically.

Feinstein and Eden's book is comprehensive, providing a rich tapestry of information that spans the essential elements of EFT. It integrates a framework grounded in contemporary psychology, an instructional approach to learning EFT, articulate explanations of the technique's components, and actionable advice for practical application. These elements are vividly brought to life through case histories, making the methodology not only accessible to lay readers but also highly relevant to professionals in the field of healing.

One of the book's unique features is the interactive way in which its case histories were developed. The content was honed with input from people who were actively applying EFT to their personal challenges while sharing their experiences with the authors. These real-life examples offer depth and context to the book, anchoring the theoretical aspects in the reality of lived experience.

The opening chapter illuminates the impact of our guiding mental models on our behavior and perspectives, presenting a striking account of a woman who triumphed over her long-held fear of heights through tapping. This section also demystifies the tapping points, their traditional Chinese names, and their associated indications. The authors recommend that the first issue you experiment with is the degree to which tapping improves your ability to breathe deeply. They also suggest integrating gratitude into your tapping regimen, and they end the chapter with a brief summary of what happens in your brain when you tap.

Chapter 2 breaks down the phases of a typical tapping session. It uses a session performed by a therapist as an example while emphasizing that self-tapping follows a similar protocol. It takes you through each of the stages, from the type of preparation that sets you up for the highest likelihood of success to evaluating your results afterward. Rating the intensity of your distress is important because before-and-after assessments tell you whether or not tapping has been effective for your particular issue.

The protocol starts with a preparation phase in which you choose the focus of your tapping session. As master EFT practitioners recommend, the authors emphasize the importance of making your target as specific as possible. Rather than tap generally on "the nightmare divorce," for instance, you focus on a specific triggering component like "the first time he brought his new girlfriend over to the house to pick up the kids." You then rate the degree of distress you feel when bringing it to mind. First-time tappers are often astonished at how quickly their negative feelings dissipate when they get this specific.

Chapter 2 goes into depth about a vital concept in EFT called "aspects." Aspects are small pieces of a larger issue or event. For instance, being threatened physically can have many aspects—from the smell of alcohol on the perpetrator's breath, to the pressure of their hand on your body, to the sirens wailing outside, to the sinking feeling in the pit of your stomach. EFT considers each of these to be a possible way in which the body and brain encode trauma and advocates tapping on each aspect.

This chapter also explains how to test your results to see if EFT is working. For this, we turn to a standard scale used in psychology, rating the emotional intensity of the event, issue, or aspect from 0 (no intensity) to 10 (maximum intensity).

Chapter 3 is called "The Detective Work" because many EFT techniques are designed to help us uncover our underlying issues. These might be energetic blockages, subconscious objections to healing, self-protective mechanisms, or self-limiting beliefs. Any of these can render tapping—or any other therapy—ineffective.

The chapter illustrates inner conflicts by presenting a dialogue between an adult client and his fantasized 10-year-old self. Each, of course, has a very different perspective on various components of a situation in which the boy was slapped. The child is bewildered and afraid while the adult self is able to provide context, perspectives, and resources.

Part 2 of the book covers the most common issues to which tapping can be applied. These range from psychological conditions like anxiety, depression, and PTSD, to physical issues like pain and disease, to addictions and impediments to peak performance, and finally to large-scale disasters like wars, famines, floods, and earthquakes.

Part 2 starts with worry, which is a universal human problem. In an easy-to-digest single-page "Quick Fix" format, the authors show how to apply each of the phases of EFT to worry. They provide a selection of basic phrases that focus the mind on worry during the tapping, after which the reader assesses how effective tapping has been for this problem. This is followed by illustrative case histories. Other chapters also make use of the "Quick Fix" format to give readers an immediate experience of how EFT might help the condition that is the focus of the chapter.

The chapter that starts with worry then moves on to panic attacks and provides four steps for overcoming them. Finally, it introduces the use of EFT for treating PTSD, with the remarkable results of the research showing that up to 90% of sufferers experience normalization of their symptoms in 10 or fewer tapping sessions.

Chapter 5, which focuses on sadness and depression, again begins with a list of Quick Fix tapping phrases to help you get started quickly. It provides a particularly poignant case history of a 45-year-old woman whose husband left her without warning, leading to years of deepening depression. A single tapping session with a therapist brought her level of sadness way down and led to a healing dream that revealed the childhood roots of her depression.

This chapter illustrates many useful angles from which depression can be approached, from developing social connections, to finding hope, to releasing negative thoughts, to boosting your self-worth—and how to use tapping to facilitate each.

In Chapter 6, the authors explain how habits develop and emphasize that they are learned. They break down habits into their four primary components and provide a repertoire of tapping phrases for establishing desired habits as well as identifying four steps to breaking an undesirable habit. They again illustrate the techniques with evocative, vivid case histories showing the stages of recovery, the action plan to implement it, and the conditions to maintain it.

Performance, the subject of Chapter 7, is examined through the lens of EFT's growing impact in sports and other performance-related areas. The chapter interweaves tapping with established performance-enhancing techniques such as goal-setting, imagery, self-talk, and mental rehearsal, while also considering the influence of childhood mental models on adult success.

The chapter shows how the guiding models from childhood that were covered in Chapter 1 shape our performance in later life. As with other issues, identifying and neutralizing internal objections—and correcting for energy blockages—will facilitate movement toward one's goals.

In Chapter 8, the focus shifts to relationships. Drawing from their extensive experience and previous bestseller, *The Energies of Love*, Feinstein and Eden guide readers in using EFT to navigate the complexities of interpersonal connections. The chapter again opens with generic Quick Fix phrases, offering a foundation for those new to tapping, and it progresses to elaborate on the role of EFT in emotional regulation and the exploration of deep-seated patterns originating from past experiences.

The chapter illustrates several ways in which tapping helps establish healthy relationships. The first and perhaps most important is to be able to move through emotional intensity without escalation. This enables you to regulate your emotions and improves your chances of gaining perspective. You might even start noticing how your responses to your current partner are founded in childhood patterns and early wounding.

The authors also recommend tapping as a background skill to use in any emotionally charged situation. The case histories of this section are particularly vivid, as they also draw on examples from the authors' own almost 50-year relationship to show how they apply these principles in their own lives.

The book's penultimate chapter offers a poignant look at the application of EFT in the aftermath of disasters. It has helped provide resolution to survivors of Hurricane Katrina, other natural disasters, and elementary school shootings. Tapping has also been used with survivors of wars, including in Kosovo, Afghanistan, Rwanda, Ukraine, and Palestine.

Through real-world accounts, including experiences with California wildfire survivors, the authors demonstrate how EFT can offer rapid emotional relief even under the most extreme stress. They propose a four-tiered model for intervention.

The first tier emphasizes immediate relief and stabilization. The second focuses on transforming self-limiting stress response patterns that can develop after a traumatic event, and that keep victims trapped in fear, rage or anguish.

The third tier focuses on the underlying long-standing psychological challenges that may emerge as a sequel to the disaster. These include pessimism, hopelessness, and childhood deficits. Only after these first three tiers have been addressed is tapping used to apply to the fourth tier, that of promoting optimal functioning. Data show that many people evidence posttraumatic growth following a shattering life event, and tapping can facilitate this resilient outcome.

The final chapter of *Tapping* casts a visionary eye toward the future implications of energy psychology. The authors contemplate the expansive role of energy fields in holistic wellness and suggest that individual healing through energy therapies like EFT can precipitate broader societal transformation. Citing evidence that energy fields have distant effects, they conclude that cultivating positive energy can have a ripple effect that extends beyond the individual.

The end of the book is as inspiring as the beginning, reminding us that these energy fields can be changed for the greater good and that, by undertaking our own healing, we participate in the healing of the world. As cultural historian Jean Houston writes in the foreword, *Tapping* is "a stunning call to action at a time of desperate personal and collective need."

Feinstein and Eden's *Tapping* is far more than a mere instruction manual. It takes us on a moving and inspiring journey through the landscape of healing, personal transformation, empowerment, and global change. It serves both as a practical, step-by-step guide to EFT and an inspirational narrative, reminding us of our capacity to reshape not only our inner experiences but the trajectory of our planet and culture.

Dawson Church, PhD, is the editor of Energy Psychology, *founder of the National Institute for Integrative Healthcare (NIIH.org), and author of best-selling science books*, The Genie in Your Genes, Mind to Matter, *and* Bliss Brain.

The Empowerment Solution: Six Keys to Unlocking Your Full Potential with the Subsconcious Mind

Friedemann Schaub, MD, PhD

Destiny Books, 2023
Softcover, 352 pages
$24.99
ISBN: 978-1644116418

Reviewed by Carol A. Atkinson

In *The Empowerment Solution*, Friedemann Schaub invites the reader to go slow, work with the many modalities offered, and truly rewrite what he calls our "outdated owner's manual" (p. 8), which we know as our subconscious. Replacing the subconscious mind's beliefs that develop into behavior patterns allows individuals to unlock who they really are, thus living a limitless life.

> You will learn how to disentangle from the past and peel off the layers of false identities, limiting beliefs, and self-negating patterns that have prevented you from seeing and appreciating your inner brilliance. You'll reconnect with your essence, realign your thoughts, feelings, and actions with your authentic truth and open your heart to reclaim the dormant gifts and powers that reside within. (p. 7)

In order to fulfill this expansive prescription, the book is organized around patterns and modalities that can be accessed easily by the layperson and used in depth by a practitioner. Schaub provides an overview of behaviors, examples from his practice, and modalities and meditations to replace the "outdated owner's manual."

The first layer of behavioral categories encompasses two survival modes: avoiding and pleasing. These two modes protect us from threats of all sorts. Some people avoid anything and everything that may lead to hurt, whether that hurt be physical, emotional, or mental injury. Other people please as much as they can, in any way they can, often to their own detriment.

The most common survival beliefs are: I am not safe, I am not good enough, I don't belong, I am not lovable, and the world isn't a good/safe place. These types of beliefs are powerful and manifest what they preach. Schaub wrote that depression and hopelessness set in when "we realize that no matter how many people or situations we avoid and how much approval we receive, we still end up stuck in powerlessness, and unsure of who we are and whether we matter" (p. 17–18). That's when people go into a survival loop, which he describes as moving from the trigger event to memories, to beliefs, to emotions, to developing a pattern, then to loss of power, and back to a trigger event (p. 17).

> The subconscious mind developed survival patterns early in our lives when we depended entirely on the adults around us. Whether we were dealing with instability or volatility in our home or were repeatedly neglected, judged, made fun of, or punished, our subconscious carefully registered and analyzed negative messages and events to determine whether we were safe, could trust in others, and deserved to be taken care of. It didn't take significant trauma and abuse for the subconscious protector to doubt our safety. (p. 14)

That subconscious protector runs 70% of our daily lives (p. 22).

The core of the book is describing a multitude of subconscious behaviors, organized into six survival patterns, then providing modalities to help replace the stories and beliefs. These modalities are organized into what Schaub calls six keys to self-empowerment. Each of the chapters covers one of the 12 survival patterns and one of the six self-empowerment keys.

The six survival patterns are:

- Victim
    - avoidance behavior
- Invisibility
    - avoidance behavior
- Procrastinator
    - avoidance behavior
- Chameleon
    - pleasing behavior
- Helper
    - pleasing behavior
- Lover
    - pleasing behavior

And the six keys to self-empowerment are:

- Self-responsibility
    - flipping the avoidance/victim behavior
- Self-compassion
    - flipping the avoidance/invisibility behavior
- Self-reliance
    - flipping the avoidance/procrastinator behavior
- Self-reflection
    - flipping the pleasing/chameleon behavior
- Self-commitment
    - flipping the pleasing/helper behavior
- Self-love
    - flipping the pleasing/lover behavior

While the understanding of the subconscious is critical and the categories of behaviors equally critical, tapping into the modalities Shaub provides really lays bare the value of this book.

The modalities for the Victim pattern and the Self-Responsibility replacement modality are the first Shaub presents and can serve as an example of what's ahead in the remaining chapters.

The Victim pattern embraces behaviors such as living in the past, justifying misery, making the body and the emotions the enemy, or becoming the perpetrator (pp. 36–41). In so doing, the victim avoids change and taking responsibility for their life. The way to replace those behaviors is through the key of Self-Responsibility. First up, the Victim must make four empowering choices (pp. 49–50):

- Commit to wholeness and well-being, even though others have insisted the person really has no value.
- Control thoughts, feelings, beliefs, and actions.
- Be willing to grow and change.
- Become the creator of one's reality.

Once those choices are accepted, then learning to forgive becomes imperative. Forgiveness is at the heart of the Self-Responsibility modality or what is really a meditation, titled "Disentanglement: Peace and Freedom Through Self-Responsibility and Forgiveness" (p. 58). In this meditation, Schaub works directly with the subconscious, instructing this deeper mind to let go and outgrow certain people. The five steps of the meditation are:

1. Preparation: Deciding on the person to forgive/let go
2. Setting the stage: Bring that perpetrator onto an imaginary stage

3. Lessons learned—and taught: Begin to access the insights and growth opportunities the individual provided
4. Freedom through forgiveness: Here negativity is released about the perpetrator and personal power given to the perpetrator is reclaimed
5. Disentanglement: Here residual attachments are released by cutting cords

To end the section, a modality called Integration is provided. Shaub suggests writing two letters. One to the person just forgiven and the second in the voice of the perpetrator. What would the victim have liked the perpetrator to say to them? (p. 73).

This two-chapter example better uncovers the work Shaub provides in this deep book. He recommends in the opening pages to go slow and take time with each of the healing modalities. While little justice is given here to the summary of the Self-Responsibility modality, that work alone can be groundbreaking for an individual trapped in the life of a victim. Thus, his caution is clear and quite relevant. This isn't a book to read and put the shelf, as he wrote. It's a book to be lived with and worked with for some time.

Though not a detriment to the substance of the book, the way the book is organized takes some time to work through and is not well foreshadowed. For this reviewer, in order to articulate how the behaviors and modalities are organized took some effort. Only after a return to the table of contents and rereading of the introduction did the full arch of organization become clear, and with hope, faithfully explained. However, that in no way negates the depth, beauty, and sincere effort to heal that Shaub brings to this publication. It is a book that every practitioner needs on their shelf.

Carol A. Atkinson, PhD, is a professor of digital media specializing in free speech, gender in the media, and personal interests in the myriad levels of consciousness. Email: Atkinson@retiree.ucmo.edu

An Energy Healer's Book of Dying: For Caregivers and Those in Transition

Suzanne Worthley

Findhorn Press, 2020
Softcover, 176 pages
$14.99
ISBN: 978-1644110324

Reviewed by Patricia Brancoforte

An energy practitioner and healer as well as an intuitive, Suzanne Worthley shares the step-by-step energetic process experienced during the transition or death process as one returns to what she terms "the Source."

This enlightening book is divided into three parts: The first describes source energy or life force, soul contracts, and the Akashic Records, as well as an overview of energy points (the chakra system). The second section takes the reader through the nine energetic levels of transition, what happens at each level, and how a loved one and/or caregiver is able to support the individual through each stage. The third part of the book deals with the final stages of transition, farewell rituals, and the process of grieving. A summary is provided after each section, giving the reader a cohesive understanding of the information presented.

In Part 1, entitled "Life-Force Energy and the Death Process," the author states that the physical body interacts with the Source through the dimensions of light or energy points known as the chakra system. She also provides an explanation of the aura that surrounds the body.

Worthley describes the dimensions of light in terms of layers of energy that can be utilized to enrich our lives, which accordingly shut down during the process of transition. She defines the Akashic Records or "The Book of Life" as a storehouse of information for every individual living on Earth. She goes on to explain that a soul contract is an agreement made regarding what we plan on accomplishing during this lifetime, further stating that we also have soul contracts with others, including those who intend to harm us. This record is sealed once the final stages of death are complete.

Part 2, "Levels of Transition," illustrates the nine levels of transitioning back to spirit. In this section, each level is explained fully, including a definition of each, what the author as an energy healer attending to the dying sees at the time, what the person may be experiencing, and healing strategies designed for the caregiver. A personal case study followed by a summary of the material is provided for each level.

Worthley terms chakra levels 1, 3, 5, and 7 as body releases. Releasing the energy at the first chakra during the time of transition is described as shutting down of all related to Earth. Chakra 3 relates to the consciousness of what we experienced in the physical sense as it relates to humanity. The consciousness of the physical as related to the universe is released at the fifth chakra level. The seventh, she notes, is the physical as it relates to the celestial soul.

Chakras 2, 4, 6, and 8 are termed the mind releases. At the second chakra, all that the mind created regarding the planet is shut down. Chakra 4 comprises the release of all that the mind created regarding humanity. Chakra 5 is the shutting down of all that the mind created regarding the universe. Chakra 8, or the eighth level of transition, is related to the celestial soul as created by the mind. The ninth level is described as that which we create or experience as relates to both the mind and the body. Once this level is complete, no chakras remain, no auric energies remain, and the Akashic Records are sealed.

Each level is thoroughly and clearly discussed in a way that even those unfamiliar with the chakra energy system can process as they relate to those undergoing the transition back to spirit.

In Part 3, "Rituals and Goodbyes," the author gives reasons and insight as to why honoring the final goodbye is an important step in the grieving and healing process, whether the honoring is an elaborate service or something as simple as lighting a candle to commemorate the life of someone who touched us in some way. In this final section, she expands a bit upon the five stages of grief: denial, anger, bargaining, depression, and acceptance. The author ends with tips on how to cope with our sadness, along with the simple fact that every individual will have their own unique way of grieving, stating "Do it *your* own way."

An Energy Healer's Book of Dying is beautifully and compassionately written. An individual going through the loss of a loved one or someone just curious about what actually happens during the time of transitioning will find comfort as well as knowledge regarding the journey from the physical back to the energy of spirit.

Patricia Brancoforte is an author and artist who has also been an active member of the metaphysical community for over 30 years, 20 of which were spent reading and teaching the Tarot. Email: pbrancoforte@outlook.com

The Language of Emotions: What Your Feelings Are Trying to Tell You

Karla McLaren, MEd

Sounds True, 2023
Softcover, 448 pages
$22.99
ISBN: 978-1649630421

Reviewed by Carol A. Atkinson

This edition of Karla McLaren's *The Language of Emotions* is an update of the 2010 one, which gave her a decade to work with other professionals regarding emotions, expand her work with clients, and create the Dynamic Emotional Integration process that applies her understanding and knowledge of emotions. In the intervening 13 years, she also developed the Four Keys to Emotional Genius, which comprise a reframing of the emotions. Also new to this edition is an Emotional Skills Inventory and practices such as Ethical Empathic Gossip.

> In this book you'll learn how to engage directly with the gifts your emotions bring to you, and in part, you'll do that by asking questions to reveal each emotion's unique genius. (p. xi)

This is a content-dense book, much of which defies distillation.

McLaren, a survivor of childhood sexual assault that spanned several years, is open about her own out-of-control emotions, including becoming an emotional tyrant, spinning into extreme moods of anger, sadness, and suicidal urges. Her intense desire to find balance in her life drove her to work with the emotions, engaging them and in some ways playing with the emotion to let it do its work of protecting the body and mind it inhabits.

Part 1 provides a deep look into emotions and how they play a role in daily life. Part 2 deals specifically with individualized emotions, such as anger, hate, or sadness.

It is in Part 1 that McLaren provides us the Four Keys to Emotional Genius.

The first key is there are no negative or positive emotions. Labeling them, or putting them in categories called valancing, creates fear and misunderstanding. Rather than labeling or suppressing, listening to an emotion and moving directly into an emotion provides a way through.

The second key is to learn how to channel emotions. The emotions can provide us clues to our gifts and abilities when we allow ourselves to express them safely.

The third key is to understand nuance. McLaren writes that emotions arise in one of three levels of intensity: soft, medium, or intense. For example, a soft hatred may emerge as being annoyed, bristling, or irritated. A medium hatred may make itself visible through antagonizing behavior or feeling hateful or resentful. An intense hatred may show itself as being contemptuous, loathing, and righteous.

The fourth key is to identify multiple emotions. Sometimes emotions occur in the singular, other times in multiples. Being able to perceive what emotions are moving through opens the ability to work with them and understand them.

McLaren makes clear that individuals cannot work with emotions purely on the intellectual level: it takes the whole person to do so. She writes of the need to understand the elements of emotions (earth, air, water, fire).

Understanding these elements provides a ground, or support, for the emotional process work. The intellect must be able to work freely in order to translate between the elements and bring knowledge to the body's sensations, visionary spirit, earthy body, and airy mind (p. 53). The earth element is thrown out of balance by overwork or ignoring the body and can return to balance through physical activities.

The air element is out of balance if there are mental swings or an inability to think. Study, reading, learning a language, or doing puzzles or games will bring that element back into balance. When the water element is out of balance, there may be overflowing emotions or, conversely, dried-up emotions. Dance, music, art, or writing poetry are ways to bring it back into balance. Finally, the fire element is out of balance when raging or watered-down emotions dominate. To balance this fire, seek spiritual calm through religious experiences, meditation, or spiritual engagement.

At the close of Part 1 in Chapter 10, McLaren shares a portion of her healing model. In that chapter, titled "Building Your Raft: The Five Empathic Mindfulness Practices," she creates what she calls a raft to navigate through emotions, thoughts, feelings, or visions. Using these practices with the support of the four elements, emotions can be safely explored and softened. "The raft you'll create is a grounded and body-based process that you'll perform with your eyes open, your mind engaged, your emotions and visions welcome, and your body comfortable" (p. 113).

That five-part process includes (pp. 116–134):

- Getting grounded, which involves breathing techniques and anchoring deep into the earth.
- Defining boundaries encompasses the imagining of a colorful bubble that protects the whole body.
- Burning contracts is a cathartic practice, imagining a roll of parchment upon which all the substance of the emotions are blown and then burned to ashes.
- Conscious complaining is just that, finding a private spot to let go and let it all out, complaining with abandon; after which, the emotions are flowing smoothly and quietly.
- The final aspect of the raft is rejuvenation, in which a scene of great happiness or serenity is imagined and carried forward into daily life.

With those modalities practiced and understood, McLaren then brings forward in-depth reviews of the various emotions. In Part 2, McLaren breaks out the types of emotions into what she labels "families" and each family comprises a chapter. While it is unclear the differences between families and categories, these families of emotions make up nearly 250 pages of the book's whole.

The families of emotions are:

- Anger, which includes apathy and boredom, shame, guilt, and hatred
- Fear, which includes anxiety and worry, confusion, jealousy/loneliness, envy, and panic
- Sadness, which includes grief, situation depression, and suicidal urges
- Happiness, which includes, contentment, joy, stress, and resistance

Each chapter provides deeply descriptive details about the emotions and then an application of how to access the emotion and how to allow it to become an ally.

As noted, the Fear family embraces the intuition and instincts, which support the orientation to surroundings, to notice changes or be aware of hazards (p. 224). If fear is a key component of a person's behavior, then the intuition and instincts are blocked and cannot be accessed.

McLaren recommends moving through the Empathetic Mindfulness practices of grounding, creating a boundary, and contract burning to move out of the fear behavior. The modality to deal with fear is to apply the Mindfulness practices, to listen carefully to the fear: stop, listen, and access the meaning. What is creating the fear and what action should be taken? Rather than being lost in the emotion of fear and unable to act or sense anything, creating that waiting space to hear, think, and make decisions will keep the fear flowing rather than freezing it.

The positive side of fear, she writes, is being able to focus on the self, the relationship between the self and the surroundings, as well as provide the energy to deal with novel situations (p. 230). Thus, fear becomes an ally rather than an emotion to stuff down.

Overall, this book brings to the forefront the ways in which emotions steal a full way of life and how working with the emotions can provide peace and personal harmony.

Having not read the 2010 edition, the sense of this 2023 book is that the earlier edition was simply added to and expanded on, thus giving this newer edition a repetitiveness that drags the reading flow. Perhaps a working manual or a supplemental text would have provided a better way to update the concepts. This is powerful and life-changing information McLaren provides and it deserves a cleanly formatted book.

Carol A. Atkinson, PhD, is a professor of digital media specializing in free speech, gender in the media, and personal interests in the myriad levels of consciousness. Email: Atkinson@retiree.ucmo.edu

The Many Faces of Life Energy: The Common Denominator for Just About Everything—From Animal Magnetism and Phantom Limbs to Team Chemistry and Crop Circles

Rick Leskowitz

Bear & Company, 2024
Softcover, 320 pages
$22.99
ISBN: 978-1591434863

Reviewed by Dawson Church

This fascinating introduction to life energy and its healing potential brings together all of the key perspectives on the topic. Those include the extensive research on everything from the human biofield to phantom limb pain to the "flow" states experienced by athletes.

The author's engaging narrative style weaves together his personal voyage of intellectual discovery as well as the case histories of the many larger-than-life figures who dot the history of energy healing. From Franz Mesmer to Wilhelm Reich, he shows both the potential and the ridicule that energy methods have typically provoked, highlighting the biases of the western medical system.

The book also provides simple personal practices that can allow you to detect your own energy field and that of others. The text is informed by the author's half-century of practice as a psychiatrist and the wry sense of humor that has given him a bird's-eye perspective that encompasses both conventional and integrative medicine.

Experienced practitioners and fans of energy therapies will find this book to be a comprehensive summary of the field, while the engaging stories and clear analogies make it accessible to newcomers. An excellent review of the field of life energy and the ways we can engage its healing potential.

Dawson Church, PhD, is the editor of Energy Psychology, *founder of the National Institute for Integrative Healthcare (NIIH.org), and author of best-selling science books*, The Genie in Your Genes, Mind to Matter, *and* Bliss Brain.

Trusting the Dawn: How to Choose Freedom and Joy after Trauma

Mary Firestone
Sounds True, 2022
Hardcover, 192 pages
$25.99
ISBN: 978-1683649120

Reviewed by Patricia Brancoforte

My interest in this book was instantly peaked by the opening paragraphs of the first chapter, in which the author describes her traumatic experience of being trapped in her disintegrating home during the Montecito mudslide of 2018, all the while not knowing what happened to her husband and son. I related heavily to this account, as I too had experienced devastation of my property and our town from the major flooding that occurred during Hurricane Irene.

Trusting the Dawn is divided into two parts. The first, "Transformation," discusses the effects trauma has on both physical and emotional levels. Firestone explains that the fight-or-flight response is activated in response to danger, releasing adrenaline and cortisol into our bodies. When the trauma is not released, these chemicals can remain stored in the body and brain, triggering physical issues. She writes of the amygdala, the part of the brain that is activated during traumatic experiences and reactivated by later triggers. She notes that everyday things such as sounds or scents can be triggers, whether the trauma was individual or the result of communal trauma such as 9/11/21, COVID-19, or the Holocaust.

Since none of us gets through life without trauma of some sort, this book gives us insight as well as tools we can utilize to heal and positively transform in the aftermath of a traumatic experience. One such tool is shifting our language so as not to become stuck in the negative, thereby aiding in healing and developing resiliency. The author states that integration by assimilating separate aspects of a traumatic experience is the key to healing.

Part 2 contains the essence of this work, providing different therapies to aid in healing by integrating the mind, body, and spirit. Firestone states several times that healing is not a one-size-fits-all modality and that each individual needs to trust in their intuition as to what may be the best method or methods for them.

In chapters 4 through 8, the author details specific therapies. For each modality, she provides an explanation, personal experience, and resources, along with, at times, a practical exercise as well as a recommendation on who it may or may not be right for, again expressing the fact that what will work for or feel comfortable for one individual may not for another.

Therapies covered in Chapter 4 are shaking therapy which is described as a natural way to discharge fear, and yoga, a resource for mindfulness and reconnecting with the body. Chapter 5 deals with scents and the use of essential oils and flower essences. Traditional Chinese medicine is highlighted in Chapter 6, covering therapies such as acupuncture to restore energy alignment, Gua Sha for healing and beautification, and Qigong, a moving meditation to bring body, mind, and spirit back into balance.

Chapter 7 explains various clinical treatments that the author states should be undertaken under the guidance of a trained therapist or healer. Three therapies outlined are Eye Movement Desensitization and Reprocessing (EMDR), craniosacral therapy (CST), and neuro-linguistic programming (NLP). Also addressed are pharmacological treatments such as ketamine, propranolol, or MDMA therapy, all of which the author states should not be attempted without first consulting a doctor. In discussing support groups and traditional talk therapy, she shares how these forms of therapy can assist in the processing of feelings with someone with whom we feel safe and comfortable.

Mystical therapies are detailed in Chapter 8, beginning with breath work, which helps an individual tap into altered states of consciousness, thereby aiding in the release of trauma, and meditation, which quiets the brain, thereby allowing for relaxation of the body, mind, and spirit. Journaling is also discussed as a therapeutic modality, something the author notes she finds helpful in her own life. In discussing shamanism, we learn possible ways to illuminate the mind-body connection.

A section on psychological astrology gives us a quick overview of how the position of the planets as well as Chiron, the healer, shapes our personality and how planetary transits can affect events in our lives. The power of prayer, asking for divine guidance, following a traumatic event is beautifully covered in a way all can relate to, no matter what individual beliefs we may have. Sound healing, a passive way to receive healing that requires no active communication from the individual, according to Firestone, is something of benefit to anyone. Lastly, past life regression therapy was touched upon as a means of healing residual trauma from a past life.

In summary, the goal of healing, according to the author, is integration and *Trusting the Dawn* provides a variety of tools to assist the individual in integrating and thus healing trauma. The book closes with different practices to attain and maintain a healthier life. For myself, a long-time meditator, I have now successfully added Qigong to my daily routine. I highly recommend this book for anyone who desires a few new techniques or modalities of treatment to aid in their journey to a happier, more serene life.

Patricia Brancoforte is an author and artist who has also been an active member of the metaphysical community for over 30 years, 20 of which were spent reading and teaching the Tarot. Email: pbrancoforte@outlook.com

AGING

Multi-discrimination exposure and biological aging: Results from the Midlife in the United States study

Cuevas, A. G., Cole, S. W., Belsky, D. W., McSorley, A. M., Shon, J. M., & Chang, V. W. (2024). Multi-discrimination exposure and biological aging: Results from the Midlife in the United States study. *Brain, Behavior, & Immunity-Health*, 100774. doi:10.1016/j.bbih.2024.1000774

Abstract

Discrimination is a social determinant of health and health disparities for which the biological mechanisms remain poorly understood. This study investigated the hypothesis that discrimination contributes to poor health outcomes by accelerating biological processes of aging. We analyzed survey and blood DNA methylation data from the Midlife in the United States (MIDUS) study ($N = 1967$). We used linear regression analysis to test associations of everyday, major, and workplace discrimination with biological aging measured by the DunedinPACE, PhenoAge, and GrimAge2 epigenetic clocks. MIDUS participants who reported more discrimination tended to exhibit a faster pace of aging and older biological age as compared to peers who reported less discrimination. Effect-sizes for associations tended to be larger for the DunedinPACE pace-of-aging clock (effect-size range $r = 0.1$–0.2) as compared with the PhenoAge and GrimAge2 biological-age clocks (effect-sizes $r < 0.1$) and for experiences of everyday and major discrimination as compared with workplace discrimination. Smoking status and body-mass index accounted for roughly half of observed association between discrimination and biological aging. Reports of discrimination were more strongly associated with accelerated biological aging among White as compared with Black participants, although Black participants reported more discrimination overall and tended to exhibit older biological age and faster biological aging. Findings support the hypothesis that experiences of interpersonal discrimination contribute to accelerated biological aging and suggest that structural and individual-level interventions to reduce discrimination and promote adaptive coping have potential to support healthy aging and build health equity.

Sleep and subjective age: Protect your sleep if you want to feel young

Balter, L. J., & Axelsson, J. (2024). Sleep and subjective age: Protect your sleep if you want to feel young. *Proceedings of the Royal Society B, 291*(2019), 20240171. doi:10.1098/rspb.2024.0171

Abstract

The current studies examined the impact of insufficient sleep and sleepiness on the subjective experience of age. Study 1, a cross-sectional study of 429 participants (282 females (66%), 144 males, 3 other gender; age range 18–70), showed that for each additional day of insufficient sleep in the last 30 days, subjective age increased by 0.23 years. Study 2, an experimental crossover sleep restriction study ($n = 186$; 102 females (55%), 84 males; age range 18–46), showed that two nights of sleep restriction (4 h in bed per night) made people feel 4.44 years older compared to sleep saturation (9 h in bed per night). Additionally, moving from feeling extremely alert (Karolinska Sleepiness Scale [KSS] score of 1) to feeling extremely sleepy (KSS score of 9) was associated with feeling 10 years older in both studies. These findings provide compelling support for insufficient sleep and sleepiness to exert a substantial influence on how old we feel, and that safeguarding sleep is probably a key factor in feeling young.

Personality traits and cognitive reserve–high openness benefits cognition in the presence of age-related brain changes

Coors, A., Lee, S., Habeck, C., & Stern, Y. (2024). Personality traits and cognitive reserve–high openness benefits cognition in the presence of age-related brain changes. *Neurobiology of Aging, 137*, 38–46. doi:10.1016/j.neurobiolaging

Abstract

Cognitive reserve explains differential susceptibility of cognitive performance to neuropathology. We investigated whether certain personality traits underlie cognitive reserve and are accordingly associated with better cognition and less cognitive decline in the presence of age-related brain changes. We included healthy adults aged 19–80 years for cross-sectional ($N = 399$) and longitudinal ($N = 273$, mean follow-up time = 5 years, $SD = 0.7$ years) analyses. Assessment of the BIG5 personality traits openness, conscientiousness, extraversion, agreeableness, and neuroticism was questionnaire-based. Each cognitive domain (perceptual speed, memory, fluid reasoning, vocabulary) was measured with up to six tasks. Cognitive domain-specific brain status variables were obtained by combining 77 structural brain measures into single scores using elastic net regularization. These brain status variables explained up to 43.1% of the variance in cognitive performance. We found that higher openness was associated with higher fluid reasoning and better vocabulary after controlling for brain status, age, and sex. Further, lower brain status was associated with a greater decline in perceptual speed only in individuals with low openness. We conclude that high openness benefits cognitive reserve.

The effects of genetic and modifiable risk factors on brain regions vulnerable to ageing and disease

Manuello, J., Min, J., McCarthy, P., Alfaro-Almagro, F., Lee, S., Smith, S., … Douaud, G. (2024). The effects of genetic and modifiable risk factors on brain regions vulnerable to ageing and disease. *Nature Communications, 15*(1), 2576. doi:10.1038/s41467-024-46344-2

Abstract

We have previously identified a network of higher-order brain regions particularly vulnerable to the ageing process, schizophrenia, and Alzheimer's disease. However, it remains unknown what the genetic influences on this fragile brain network are and whether it can be altered by the most common modifiable risk factors for dementia. Here, in ~40,000 UK Biobank participants, we first show significant genome-wide associations between this brain network and seven genetic clusters implicated in cardiovascular deaths, schizophrenia, Alzheimer's, and Parkinson's disease, and with the two antigens of the XG blood group located in the pseudoautosomal region of the sex chromosomes. We further reveal that the most deleterious modifiable risk factors for this vulnerable brain network are diabetes, nitrogen dioxide (a proxy for traffic-related air pollution), and alcohol intake frequency. The extent of these associations was uncovered by examining these modifiable risk factors in a single model to assess the unique contribution of each on the vulnerable brain network, above and beyond the dominating effects of age and sex. These results provide a comprehensive picture of the role played by genetic and modifiable risk factors on these fragile parts of the brain.

Multisensory gamma stimulation promotes glymphatic clearance of amyloid

Murdock, M. H., Yang, C. Y., Sun, N., Pao, P. C., Blanco-Duque, C., Kahn, M. C., … Tsai, L. H. (2024). Multisensory gamma stimulation promotes glymphatic clearance of amyloid. *Nature, 627*(8002), 149–156. doi:10.1038/s41586-024-07132-6

Abstract

The glymphatic movement of fluid through the brain removes metabolic waste. Noninvasive 40 Hz stimulation promotes 40 Hz neural activity in multiple brain regions and attenuates pathology in mouse models of Alzheimer's disease. Here we show that multisensory gamma stimulation promotes the influx of cerebrospinal fluid and the efflux of interstitial fluid in the cortex of the 5XFAD mouse model of Alzheimer's disease. Influx of cerebrospinal fluid was associated with increased aquaporin-4 polarization along astrocytic endfeet and dilated meningeal lymphatic vessels. Inhibiting glymphatic clearance abolished the removal of amyloid by multisensory 40 Hz stimulation. Using chemogenetic manipulation and a genetically encoded sensor for neuropeptide signaling, we found that vasoactive intestinal peptide interneurons facilitate glymphatic clearance by regulating arterial pulsatility. Our findings establish novel mechanisms that recruit the glymphatic system to remove brain amyloid.

ANXIETY/DEPRESSION

Sudden gains in face-to-face and internet-based cognitive therapy for social anxiety disorder

Thew, G. R., Ehlers, A., & Clark, D. M. (2023). Sudden gains in face-to-face and internet-based cognitive therapy for social anxiety disorder. *Behaviour Research and Therapy, 166*, 104334. doi:10.1016/j.brat.2023.104334

Abstract

Sudden gains are large and stable decreases in clinical symptoms between consecutive therapy sessions. This work examined the frequency and possible determinants of sudden gains in cognitive therapy (CT) for social anxiety disorder, comparing face-to-face (CT) and internet-based (iCT) formats of treatment delivery. Data from 99 participants from a randomized controlled trial were analyzed. The frequency of sudden gains was high: 64% and 51% of participants experienced a sudden gain in CT and iCT respectively. Having a sudden gain was associated with lower social anxiety symptoms at posttreatment and follow-up. There was evidence of reductions in negative social cognitions and self-focused attention immediately prior to the sudden gain, contrasting with no prior reductions in depression symptoms. Ratings of session videotapes in CT showed that clients' statements indicated greater generalized learning in sessions immediately prior to gains, compared to control sessions. This may suggest a role for generalized learning in facilitating these large symptom reductions. There were no significant differences in results between the CT and iCT treatment formats, suggesting that the therapy content appears to play a more important role in determining participants' large symptom improvements than the medium of treatment delivery.

Excitatory and inhibitory neurochemical markers of anxiety in young females

Johnstone, N., & Kadosh, K. C. (2024). Excitatory and inhibitory neurochemical markers of anxiety in young females. *Developmental Cognitive Neuroscience, 66*, 101363. doi:10.1016/j.dcn.2024.101363

Abstract

Between the ages of 10 and 25 years, the maturing brain is sensitive to a multitude of changes, including neurochemical variations in metabolites. Of the different metabolites, gamma-aminobutyric acid (GABA) has long been linked neurobiologically to anxiety symptomology, which begins to manifest in adolescence. To prevent persistent anxiety difficulties into adulthood, we need to understand the maturational trajectories of neurochemicals and how these relate to anxiety levels during this sensitive period. We used magnetic resonance spectroscopy in a sample of younger (aged 10–11) and older (aged 18–25) females to estimate GABA and glutamate levels in brain regions linked to emotion regulation processing, as well as a conceptually distinct control region. Within the Bayesian framework, we found that GABA increased and glutamate decreased with age, negative associations between anxiety and glutamate and GABA ratios in the dorsolateral prefrontal cortex, and a positive relationship of GABA with anxiety levels. The results support the neural over-inhibition hypothesis of anxiety based on GABAergic activity.

Climate change anxiety positively predicts antenatal distress in expectant female parents

Lykins, A. D., Bonich, M., Sundaraja, C., & Cosh, S. (2024). Climate change anxiety positively predicts antenatal distress in expectant female parents. *Journal of Anxiety Disorders, 101*, 102801. doi:10.1016/j.janxdis.2023.102801

Abstract
Clinical and subclinical levels of anxiety and depression are common experiences during pregnancy for expectant women; however, despite rising awareness of significant climate change anxiety around the world, the extent to which this particular type of anxiety may be contributing to overall antenatal psychological distress is currently unknown. Furthermore, the content of concerns that expectant women may have for their existing or future children remains unexplored. To address this gap in knowledge, 103 expectant Australian women completed standardized assessments of antenatal worry and depression, climate change anxiety, and perceived distance to climate change, and responded to several open-ended questions on concerns they had for their children. Results indicated that climate change anxiety accounted for significant percentages of variance in both antenatal worry and depression scores and, unexpectedly, neither child number nor perceived distance to climate change moderated these relationships. Content analysis of qualitative data highlighted the significant health-related anxieties for participants' children related to climate change (e.g., disease, exposure to extreme weather events, food/water insecurity). Given the escalating nature of climate change, further investigation of this relatively new stressor contributing to the experience of anxiety and distress, particularly in uniquely vulnerable groups such as expectant women, is urgently needed.

Effect of exercise for depression: Systematic review and network meta-analysis of randomised controlled trials

Noetel, M., Sanders, T., Gallardo-Gómez, D., Taylor, P., del Pozo Cruz, B., Van Den Hoek, D., … Lonsdale, C. (2024). Effect of exercise for depression: Systematic review and network meta-analysis of randomised controlled trials. *BMJ, 384*, e075847. doi:10.1136/bmj-2023-075847

Abstract
Objective: To identify the optimal dose and modality of exercise for treating major depressive disorder, compared with psychotherapy, antidepressants, and control conditions.

Design: Systematic review and network meta-analysis.

Methods: Screening, data extraction, coding, and risk of bias assessment were performed independently and in duplicate. Bayesian arm based, multilevel network meta-analyses were performed for the primary analyses. Quality of the evidence for each arm was graded using the confidence in network meta-analysis (CINeMA) online tool.

Data sources: Cochrane Library, Medline, Embase, SPORTDiscus, and PsycINFO databases.

Eligibility criteria for selecting studies: Any randomized trial with exercise arms for participants meeting clinical cut-offs for major depression.

Results: 218 unique studies with a total of 495 arms and 14,170 participants were included. Compared with active controls (e.g., usual care, placebo tablet), moderate reductions in depression were found for walking or jogging (n = 1210, κ = 51, Hedges' g –0.62, 95% credible interval –0.80 to –0.45), yoga (n = 1047, κ = 33, g –0.55, –0.73 to –0.36), strength training (n = 643, κ = 22, g –0.49, –0.69 to –0.29), mixed aerobic exercises (n = 1286, κ = 51, g –0.43, –0.61 to –0.24), and tai chi or qigong (n = 343, κ = 12, g –0.42, –0.65 to –0.21). The effects of exercise were proportional to the intensity prescribed. Strength training and yoga appeared to be the most acceptable modalities. Results appeared robust to publication bias, but only one study met the Cochrane criteria for low risk of bias. As a result, confidence in accordance with CINeMA was low for walking or jogging and very low for other treatments.

Conclusions: Exercise is an effective treatment for depression, with walking or jogging, yoga, and strength training more effective than other exercises, particularly when intense. Yoga and strength training were well tolerated compared with other treatments. Exercise appeared equally effective for people with and without comorbidities and with different baseline levels of depression. To mitigate expectancy effects, future studies could aim to blind participants and staff. These forms of exercise could be considered alongside psychotherapy and antidepressants as core treatments for depression.

Interplay of early negative life events, development of orbitofrontal cortical thickness and depression in young adulthood

Backhausen, L. L., Granzow, J., Fröhner, J. H., Artiges, E., Paillère-Martinot, M. L., Lemaître, H., ... IMAGEN Consortium. (2024). Interplay of early negative life events, development of orbitofrontal cortical thickness and depression in young adulthood. *JCPP Advances, 4*(1), e12210. doi:10.1002/jcv2.12210

Abstract

Background: Early negative life events (NLEs) have long-lasting influences on neurodevelopment and psychopathology. Reduced orbitofrontal cortex (OFC) thickness was frequently associated with NLEs and depressive symptoms. OFC thinning might mediate the effect of NLEs on depressive symptoms, although few longitudinal studies exist. Using a complete longitudinal design with four time points, we examined whether NLEs during childhood and early adolescence predict depressive symptoms in young adulthood through accelerated OFC thinning across adolescence.

Methods: We acquired structural MRI from 321 participants at two sites across four time points from ages 14 to 22. We measured NLEs with the Life Events Questionnaire at the first time point and depressive symptoms with the Center for Epidemiologic Studies Depression Scale at the fourth time point. Modeling latent growth curves, we tested whether OFC thinning mediates the effect of NLEs on depressive symptoms.

Results: A higher burden of NLEs, a thicker OFC at the age of 14, and an accelerated OFC thinning across adolescence predicted young adults' depressive symptoms. We did not identify an effect of NLEs on OFC thickness nor OFC thickness mediating effects of NLEs on depressive symptoms.

Conclusions: Using a complete longitudinal design with four waves, we show that NLEs in childhood and early adolescence predict depressive symptoms in the long term. Results indicate that an accelerated OFC thinning may precede depressive symptoms. Assessment of early additionally to acute NLEs and neurodevelopment may be warranted in clinical settings to identify risk factors for depression.

ARTIFICIAL INTELLIGENCE (AI)

Identifying depression and its determinants upon initiating treatment: ChatGPT versus primary care physicians

Levkovich, I., & Elyoseph, Z. (2023). Identifying depression and its determinants upon initiating treatment: ChatGPT versus primary care physicians. *Family Medicine and Community Health, 11*(4), e002391. doi:10.1136/fmch-2023-002391

Abstract

Objective: To compare evaluations of depressive episodes and suggested treatment protocols generated by Chat Generative Pretrained Transformer (ChatGPT)-3 and ChatGPT-4 with the recommendations of primary care physicians.

Methods: Vignettes were input to the ChatGPT interface. These vignettes focused primarily on hypothetical patients with symptoms of depression during initial consultations. The creators of these vignettes meticulously designed eight distinct versions in which they systematically varied patient attributes (sex, socioeconomic status [blue collar worker or white collar worker] and depression severity [mild or severe]). Each variant was subsequently introduced into ChatGPT-3.5 and ChatGPT-4. Each vignette was repeated 10 times to ensure consistency and reliability of the ChatGPT responses.

Results: For mild depression, ChatGPT-3.5 and ChatGPT-4 recommended psychotherapy in 95.0% and 97.5% of cases, respectively. Primary care physicians, however, recommended psychotherapy in only 4.3% of cases. For severe cases, ChatGPT favored an approach that combined psychotherapy, while primary care physicians recommended a combined approach. The pharmacological recommendations of ChatGPT-3.5 and ChatGPT-4 showed a preference for exclusive use of antidepressants (74% and 68%, respectively), in contrast with primary care physicians, who typically recommended a mix of antidepressants and anxiolytics/hypnotics (67.4%). Unlike primary care physicians, ChatGPT showed no gender or socioeconomic biases in its recommendations.

Conclusion: ChatGPT-3.5 and ChatGPT-4 aligned well with accepted guidelines for managing mild and severe depression, without showing the gender or socioeconomic biases observed among primary care physicians. Despite the suggested potential benefit of using artificial intelligence (AI) chatbots like ChatGPT to enhance clinical decision making, further research is needed to refine AI recommendations for severe cases and to consider potential risks and ethical issues.

Conversational AI and equity through assessing GPT-3's communication with diverse social groups on contentious topics

Chen, K., Shao, A., Burapacheep, J., & Li, Y. (2024). Conversational AI and equity through assessing GPT-3's communication with diverse social groups on contentious topics. *Scientific Reports, 14*(1), 1561. doi:10.1038/s41598-024-51969-w

Abstract

Autoregressive language models, which use deep learning to produce human-like texts, have surged in prevalence. Despite advances in these models, concerns arise about their equity across diverse populations. While AI fairness is discussed widely, metrics to measure equity in dialogue systems are lacking. This paper presents a framework, rooted in deliberative democracy and science communication studies, to evaluate equity in human-AI communication. Using it, we conducted an algorithm auditing study to examine how GPT-3 responded to different populations who vary in sociodemographic backgrounds and viewpoints on crucial science and social issues: climate change and the Black Lives Matter (BLM) movement. We analyzed 20,000 dialogues with 3,290 participants differing in gender, race, education, and opinions. We found a substantively worse user experience among the opinion minority groups (e.g., climate deniers, racists) and the education minority groups; however, these groups changed attitudes toward supporting BLM and climate change efforts much more compared to other social groups after the chat. GPT-3 used more negative expressions when responding to the education and opinion minority groups. We discuss the social-technological implications of our findings for a conversational AI system that centralizes diversity, equity, and inclusion.

Seeing is no longer believing: A survey on the state of deepfakes, AI-generated humans, and other nonveridical media

Pocol, A., Istead, L., Siu, S., Mokhtari, S., & Kodeiri, S. (2023, August). Seeing is no longer believing: A survey on the state of deepfakes, AI-generated humans, and other nonveridical media. In *Computer Graphics International Conference* (pp. 427–440). Cham: Springer Nature Switzerland. doi:10.1007/978-3-031-50072-5_34

Abstract

Did you see that crazy photo of Chris Hemsworth wearing a gorgeous, blue ballgown? What about the leaked photo of Bernie Sanders dancing with Sarah Palin? If these don't sound familiar, it's because these events never happened—but with text-to-image generators and deepfake AI technologies, it is effortless for anyone to produce such images. Over the last decade, there has been an explosive rise in research papers, as well as tool development and usage, dedicated to deepfakes, text-to-image generation, and image synthesis. These tools provide users with great creative power, but with that power comes "great responsibility;" it is just as easy to produce nefarious and misleading content as it is to produce comedic or artistic content. Therefore, given the recent advances in the field, it is important to assess the impact they may have. In this paper, we conduct meta-research on deepfakes to visualize the evolution of these tools and paper publications. We also identify key authors, research institutions, and papers based on bibliometric data. Finally, we conduct a survey that tests the ability of participants to distinguish photos of real people from fake, AI-generated images of people. Based on our meta-research, survey, and background study, we conclude that humans are falling behind in the race to keep up with AI, and we must be conscious of the societal impact.

Is it harmful or helpful? Examining the causes and consequences of generative AI usage among university students

Abbas, M., Jam, F. A., & Khan, T. I. (2024). Is it harmful or helpful? Examining the causes and consequences of generative AI usage among university students. *International Journal of Educational Technology in Higher Education, 21*(1), 10. doi:10.1186/s41239-024-00444-7

Abstract
While the discussion on generative artificial intelligence, such as ChatGPT, is making waves in academia and the popular press, there is a need for more insight into the use of ChatGPT among students and the potential harmful or beneficial consequences associated with its usage. Using samples from two studies, the current research examined the causes and consequences of ChatGPT usage among university students. Study 1 developed and validated an eight-item scale to measure ChatGPT usage by conducting a survey among university students ($N = 165$). Study 2 used a three-wave time-lagged design to collect data from university students ($N = 494$) to further validate the scale and test the study's hypotheses. Study 2 also examined the effects of academic workload, academic time pressure, sensitivity to rewards, and sensitivity to quality on ChatGPT usage. Study 2 further examined the effects of ChatGPT usage on students' levels of procrastination, memory loss, and academic performance. Study 1 provided evidence for the validity and reliability of the ChatGPT usage scale. Furthermore, study 2 revealed that when students faced higher academic workload and time pressure, they were more likely to use ChatGPT. In contrast, students who were sensitive to rewards were less likely to use ChatGPT. Not surprisingly, use of ChatGPT was likely to develop tendencies for procrastination and memory loss and dampen the students' academic performance. Finally, academic workload, time pressure, and sensitivity to rewards had indirect effects on students' outcomes through ChatGPT usage.

Challenges and opportunities in translating ethical AI principles into practice for children

Wang, G., Zhao, J., Van Kleek, M., & Shadbolt, N. (2024). Challenges and opportunities in translating ethical AI principles into practice for children. *Nature Machine Intelligence, 6*, 265–270. doi:10.1038/s42256-024-00805-x

Abstract
AI systems are becoming increasingly pervasive within children's devices, apps, and services. The concern over a world where AI systems are deployed unchecked has raised burning questions about the impact, governance, and accountability of these technologies. Although recent effort on AI ethics has converged into growing consensus on a set of high-level ethical AI principles, engagement with children's issues is still limited and even less is known about how to effectively apply them in practice for children. This perspective first maps the current global landscape of existing ethics guidelines for AI and analyzes their correlation with children. We then critically assess the strategies and recommendations proposed by current AI ethics initiatives, identifying the critical challenges in translating such ethical AI principles into practice for children. Finally, we tentatively map out several suggestions regarding embedding ethics into the development and governance of AI for children.

On Scene Injury Severity Prediction (OSISP) model for trauma developed using the Swedish Trauma Registry

Bakidou, A., Caragounis, E. C., Andersson Hagiwara, M., Jonsson, A., Sjöqvist, B. A., & Candefjord, S. (2023). On Scene Injury Severity Prediction (OSISP) model for trauma developed using the Swedish Trauma Registry. *BMC Medical Informatics and Decision Making, 23*(1), 206. doi:10.1186/s12911-023-02290-5

Abstract

Background: Providing optimal care for trauma, the leading cause of death for young adults, remains a challenge (e.g., due to field triage limitations in assessing a patient's condition and deciding on transport destination). Data-driven On Scene Injury Severity Prediction (OSISP) models for motor vehicle crashes have shown potential for providing real-time decision support. The objective of this study is therefore to evaluate if an artificial intelligence (AI) based clinical decision support system can identify severely injured trauma patients in the prehospital setting.

Methods: The Swedish Trauma Registry was used to train and validate five models—Logistic Regression, Random Forest, XGBoost, Support Vector Machine and Artificial Neural Network—in a stratified 10-fold cross validation setting and hold-out analysis. The models performed binary classification of the New Injury Severity Score and were evaluated using accuracy metrics, area under the receiver operating characteristic curve (AUC) and Precision-Recall curve (AUCPR), and under- and over-triage rates.

Results: There were 75,602 registrations between 2013 and 2020 and 47,357 (62.6%) remained after eligibility criteria were applied. Models were based on 21 predictors, including injury location. From the clinical outcome, about 40% of patients were under-triaged and 46% were over-triaged. Models demonstrated potential for improved triaging and yielded AUC between 0.80-0.89 and AUCPR between 0.43 and 0.62.

Conclusions: AI-based OSISP models have potential to provide support during assessment of injury severity. The findings may be used for developing tools to complement field triage protocols, with potential to improve prehospital trauma care and thereby reduce morbidity and mortality for a large patient population.

ATTITUDES/BELIEFS

Fact-opinion differentiation

Mettler, M., & Mondak, J. J. (2024). Fact-opinion differentiation. *Harvard Kennedy School Misinformation Review, 5*(2). doi:10.37016/mr-2020-136

Abstract

Statements of fact can be proved or disproved with objective evidence, whereas statements of opinion depend on personal values and preferences. Distinguishing between these types of statements contributes to information competence. Conversely, failure at fact-opinion differentiation potentially brings resistance to corrections of misinformation and susceptibility to manipulation. Our analyses show that on fact-opinion differentiation tasks, unsystematic mistakes and mistakes emanating from partisan bias occur at higher rates than accurate responses. Accuracy increases with political sophistication. Affective partisan polarization promotes systematic partisan error: As views grow more polarized, partisans increasingly see their side as holding facts and the opposing side as holding opinions.

"I one-hundred thousand percent blame it on QAnon": The impact of QAnon belief on interpersonal relationships

Mastroni, L., & Mooney, R. (2023). "I one-hundred thousand percent blame it on QAnon": The impact of QAnon belief on interpersonal relationships. *Journal of Social and Personal Relationships.* doi:10.1177/02654075241246124

Abstract

Conspiracy beliefs have been found to have negative real-world consequences that can impact interpersonal relationships; however, this remains an under-researched area. With the current popularity of conspiracy movements such as QAnon, more research into these phenomena is necessary. The present research therefore aimed to explore the impact of QAnon belief on interpersonal relationships. Fifteen participants aged 21–54 ($M = 41$) with a QAnon-affiliated loved one were interviewed about how QAnon has changed their relationship. Using thematic analysis, four main themes were identified: Malignant Q, Distance, Qonflict, and Attempts at Healing. Participants characterized QAnon as a malignant force in their relationships and communicated with their loved ones less as a result. Although QAnon was a source of conflict and tension for all participants, they were motivated to understand their loved ones. Most participants who still had relationships with their loved ones were motivated to heal or maintain their relationships, while those who no longer did had previously tried many different strategies to save their relationships. These findings provide greater insight into how QAnon can impact relationships, offering fruitful directions for future research examining how individuals can heal from QAnon-afflicted relationships.

Let it go: How exaggerating the reputational costs of revealing negative information encourages secrecy in relationships

Kardas, M., Kumar, A., & Epley, N. (2023). Let it go: How exaggerating the reputational costs of revealing negative information encourages secrecy in relationships. *Journal of Personality and Social Psychology.* doi:10.1037/pspi0000441

Abstract

Keeping negative interpersonal secrets can diminish well-being, yet people nevertheless keep negative information secret from friends, family, and loved ones to protect their own reputations. Twelve experiments suggest these reputational concerns are systematically miscalibrated, creating a misplaced barrier to honesty in relationships. In hypothetical scenarios (Experiments 1, S1, and S2), laboratory experiments (Experiments 2 and 6), and field settings (Experiments 3 and 4), those who imagined revealing, or who actually revealed, negative information they were keeping secret expected to be judged significantly more harshly than recipients expected to judge, or actually judged, them. We theorized that revealers' pessimistic expectations stem not only from the cognitive accessibility of negative information (Experiment S3) but also from a perspective gap such that the negative outcomes of disclosing this information, compared to positive outcomes, are more accessible for prospective revealers than for recipients. Consistent with this mechanism, revealers' expectations were better calibrated when directed to focus on positive thoughts or when they considered revealing positive information (Experiments 5, 6, and S4). Revealers' miscalibrated expectations matter because they can guide decisions about whether to reveal information or conceal it as a secret (Experiment S5). As predicted, calibrating revealers' expectations increased their willingness to reveal negative information to others (Experiment 7), suggesting that miscalibrated fears of others' judgment create a misplaced barrier to honesty in relationships. Overestimating the reputational costs of disclosing negative information might leave people carrying a heavier burden of secrecy than would be optimal for their own well-being.

BRAIN/COGNITION

Mindfulness enhances cognitive functioning: A meta-analysis of 111 randomized controlled trials

Zainal, N. H., & Newman, M. G. (2023). Mindfulness enhances cognitive functioning: A meta-analysis of 111 randomized controlled trials. *Health Psychology Review, 18*(2), 369–395. doi:10.1080/17437199.2023.2248222

Abstract

Background: Currently no comprehensive meta-analysis of mindfulness-based interventions (MBIs) efficacy on global and unique cognitive subdomains exist.

Method: Examined the effects of MBIs on global cognition and 15 cognitive subdomains.

Inclusion criteria: Meditation naïve participants; randomized controlled trial; outcome included one objective or subjective cognitive functioning measure; primary focus was teaching mindfulness skills. Exclusion criteria: inadequate data; one-session; control condition contained any MBI component. Robust variance estimation and moderator analyses controlling for presence of treatment fidelity were conducted.

Results: 111 RCTs (n = 9,538) met eligibility criteria. MBIs had small-to-moderate significant effects on global cognition, executive attention, working memory accuracy, inhibition accuracy, shifting accuracy, sustained attention, and subjective cognitive functioning (vs. waitlist/no-treatment, g = 0.257–0.643; vs. active controls, g = 0.192–0.394). MBIs did not impact executive functioning (EF) latency indices, verbal fluency, processing speed, episodic memory, and cognitive error. Treatment effects were stronger for those with elevated psychiatric symptoms vs. healthy controls, and medical samples, studies with complete-case (vs. intention-to-treat) analysis, face-to-face (vs. self-guided) delivery, and non-standard (vs. standard MBI).

Conclusion: MBIs consistently yielded small-to-moderate yet practically meaningful effect sizes on global cognition and six cognitive subdomains that captured accuracy vs. latency-based indices of EF and sustained accuracy.

Diverse adolescents' transcendent thinking predicts young adult psychosocial outcomes via brain network development

Gotlieb, R. J., Yang, X. F., & Immordino-Yang, M. H. (2024). Diverse adolescents' transcendent thinking predicts young adult psychosocial outcomes via brain network development. *Scientific Reports, 14*(1), 6254. doi:10.1038/s41598-024-56800-0

Abstract

Developmental scientists have long described mid-adolescents' emerging capacities to make deep meaning about the social world and self, here called transcendent thinking, as a hallmark developmental stage. In this 5-year longitudinal study, sixty-five 14–18 years-old youths' proclivities to grapple psychologically with the ethical, systems-level, and personal implications of social stories, predicted future increases in the coordination of two key brain networks: the default-mode network, involved in reflective, autobiographical and free-form thinking; and the executive control network, involved in effortful, focused thinking. Findings were independent of IQ, ethnicity, and socioeconomic background. This neural development predicted late-adolescent identity development, which predicted young-adult self-liking and relationship satisfaction, in a developmental cascade. The findings reveal a novel predictor of mid-adolescents' neural development and suggest the importance of attending to adolescents' proclivities to engage agentically with complex perspectives and emotions on the social and personal relevance of issues, such as through civically minded educational approaches.

Social bonding in groups of humans selectively increases inter-status information exchange and prefrontal neural synchronization

Ni, J., Yang, J., & Ma, Y. (2024). Social bonding in groups of humans selectively increases inter-status information exchange and prefrontal neural synchronization. *PloS Biology, 22*(3), e3002545. doi:10.1371/journal.pbio.3002545

Abstract

Social groups in various social species are organized with hierarchical structures that shape group dynamics and the nature of within-group interactions. In-group social bonding, exemplified by grooming behaviors among animals and collective rituals and team-building activities in human societies, is recognized as a practical adaptive strategy to foster group harmony and stabilize hierarchical structures in both human and nonhuman animal groups. However, the neurocognitive mechanisms underlying the effects of social bonding on hierarchical groups remain largely unexplored. Here, we conducted simultaneous neural recordings on human participants engaged in group communications within small hierarchical groups ($n = 528$, organized into 176 three-person groups) to investigate how social bonding influenced hierarchical interactions and neural synchronizations. We differentiated interpersonal interactions between individuals of different (inter-status) or same (intra-status) social status and observed distinct effects of social bonding on inter-status and intra-status interactions. Specifically, social bonding selectively increased frequent and rapid information exchange and prefrontal neural synchronization for inter-status dyads but not intra-status dyads. Furthermore, social bonding facilitated unidirectional neural alignment from group leader to followers, enabling group leaders to predictively align their prefrontal activity with that of followers. These findings provide insights into how social bonding influences hierarchical dynamics and neural synchronization while highlighting the role of social status in shaping the strength and nature of social bonding experiences in human groups.

Functional characterization of the language network of polyglots and hyperpolyglots with precision fMRI

Malik-Moraleda, S., Jouravlev, O., Taliaferro, M., Mineroff, Z., Cucu, T., Mahowald, K., … Fedorenko, E. (2024). Functional characterization of the language network of polyglots and hyperpolyglots with precision fMRI. *Cerebral Cortex, 34*(3), bhae049. doi:10.1093/cercor/bhae049

Abstract

How do polyglots—individuals who speak five or more languages—process their languages, and what can this population tell us about the language system? Using fMRI, we identified the language network in each of 34 polyglots (including 16 hyperpolyglots with knowledge of 10+ languages) and examined its response to the native language, non-native languages of varying proficiency, and unfamiliar languages. All language conditions engaged all areas of the language network relative to a control condition. Languages that participants rated as higher proficiency elicited stronger responses, except for the native language, which elicited a similar or lower response than a non-native language of similar proficiency. Furthermore, unfamiliar languages that were typologically related to the participants' high-to-moderate-proficiency languages elicited a stronger response than unfamiliar unrelated languages. The results suggest that the language network's response magnitude scales with the degree of engagement of linguistic computations (e.g., related to lexical access and syntactic-structure building). We also replicated a prior finding of weaker responses to native language in polyglots than non-polyglot bilinguals. These results contribute to our understanding of how multiple languages coexist within a single brain and provide new evidence that the language network responds more strongly to stimuli that more fully engage linguistic computations.

Attention deficits linked with proclivity to explore while foraging

Barack, D. L., Ludwig, V. U., Parodi, F., Ahmed, N., Brannon, E. M., Ramakrishnan, A., & Platt, M. L. (2024). Attention deficits linked with proclivity to explore while foraging. *Proceedings of the Royal Society B, 291*(2017), 20222584. doi:10.1098/rspb.2022.2584

Abstract

All mobile organisms forage for resources, choosing how and when to search for new opportunities by comparing current returns with the average for the environment. In humans, nomadic lifestyles favoring exploration have been associated with genetic mutations implicated in attention deficit hyperactivity disorder (ADHD), inviting the hypothesis that this condition may impact foraging decisions in the general population. Here we tested this pre-registered hypothesis by examining how human participants collected resources in an online foraging task. On every trial, participants chose either to continue to collect rewards from a depleting patch of resources or to replenish the patch. Participants also completed a well-validated ADHD self-report screening assessment at the end of sessions. Participants departed resource patches sooner when travel times between patches were shorter than when they were longer, as predicted by optimal foraging theory. Participants whose scores on the ADHD scale crossed the threshold for a positive screen departed patches significantly sooner than participants who did not meet this criterion. Participants meeting this threshold for ADHD also achieved higher reward rates than individuals who did not. Our findings suggest that ADHD attributes may confer foraging advantages in some environments and invite the possibility that this condition may reflect an adaptation favoring exploration over exploitation.

Neuronal dynamics direct cerebrospinal fluid perfusion and brain clearance

Jiang-Xie, L. F., Drieu, A., Bhasiin, K., Quintero, D., Smirnov, I., & Kipnis, J. (2024). Neuronal dynamics direct cerebrospinal fluid perfusion and brain clearance. *Nature, 627*(8002), 157–164. doi:10.1038/s41586-024-07108-6.

Abstract

The accumulation of metabolic waste is a leading cause of numerous neurological disorders, yet we still have only limited knowledge of how the brain performs self-cleansing. Here we demonstrate that neural networks synchronize individual action potentials to create large-amplitude, rhythmic, and self-perpetuating ionic waves in the interstitial fluid of the brain. These waves are a plausible mechanism to explain the correlated potentiation of the glymphatic flow1,2 through the brain parenchyma. Chemogenetic flattening of these high-energy ionic waves largely impeded cerebrospinal fluid infiltration into and clearance of molecules from the brain parenchyma. Notably, synthesized waves generated through transcranial optogenetic stimulation substantially potentiated cerebrospinal fluid-to-interstitial fluid perfusion. Our study demonstrates that neurons serve as master organizers for brain clearance. This fundamental principle introduces a new theoretical framework for the functioning of macroscopic brain waves.

An energy costly architecture of neuromodulators for human brain evolution and cognition

Castrillon, G., Epp, S., Bose, A., Fraticelli, L., Hechler, A., Belenya, R., … Riedl, V. (2023). An energy costly architecture of neuromodulators for human brain evolution and cognition. *Science Advances, 9*(50), eadi7632. doi:10.1126/sciadv.adi7632

Abstract

In comparison to other species, the human brain exhibits one of the highest energy demands relative to body metabolism. It remains unclear whether this heightened energy demand uniformly supports an enlarged brain or if specific signaling mechanisms necessitate greater energy. We hypothesized that the regional distribution of energy demands will reveal signaling strategies that have contributed to human cognitive development. We measured the energy distribution within the brain functional connectome using multimodal brain imaging and found that signaling pathways in evolutionarily expanded regions have up to 67% higher energetic costs than those in sensory-motor regions. Additionally, histology, transcriptomic data, and molecular imaging independently reveal an up-regulation of signaling at G-protein-coupled receptors in energy-demanding regions. Our findings indicate that neuromodulator activity is predominantly involved in cognitive functions, such as reading or memory processing. This study suggests that an up-regulation of neuromodulator activity, alongside increased brain size, is a crucial aspect of human brain evolution.

Phantom touch illusion, an unexpected phenomenological effect of tactile gating in the absence of tactile stimulation

Pilacinski, A., Metzler, M., & Klaes, C. (2023). Phantom touch illusion, an unexpected phenomenological effect of tactile gating in the absence of tactile stimulation. *Scientific Reports, 13*(1), 15453. doi:10.1038/s41598-023-42683-0

Abstract

We report the presence of a tingling sensation perceived during self-touch without physical stimulation. We used immersive virtual reality scenarios in which subjects touched their body using a virtual object. This touch resulted in a tingling sensation corresponding to the location touched on the virtual body. We called it "phantom touch illusion" (PTI). Interestingly, the illusion was also reported when subjects touched invisible (inferred) parts of their limb. We reason that this PTI results from tactile gating process during self-touch if there is no tactile input to suppress. The reported PTI when touching invisible body parts indicates that tactile gating is not exclusively based on vision, but rather on multi-sensory, top-down input involving body schema. This supplementary finding shows that representations of one's own body are defined top-down, beyond the available sensory information.

Attachment reminders trigger widespread synchrony across multiple brains

Shimon-Raz, O., Yeshurun, Y., Ulmer-Yaniv, A., Levinkron, A., Salomon, R., & Feldman, R. (2023). Attachment reminders trigger widespread synchrony across multiple brains. *Journal of Neuroscience, 43*(43), 7213–7225. doi:10.1523/JNEUROSCI.0026-23.2023

Abstract

Infant stimuli elicit widespread neural and behavioral response in human adults, and such massive allocation of resources attests to the evolutionary significance of the primary attachment. Here, we examined whether attachment reminders also trigger cross-brain concordance and generate greater neural uniformity, as indicated by intersubject correlation. Human mothers were imaged twice in oxytocin/placebo administration design, and stimuli included four ecological videos of a standard unfamiliar mother and infant: two infant/mother alone (Alone) and two mother-infant dyadic contexts (Social). Theory-driven analysis measured cross-brain synchrony in preregistered nodes of the parental caregiving network (PCN), which integrates subcortical structures underpinning mammalian mothering with cortical areas implicated in simulation, mentalization, and emotion regulation, and data-driven analysis assessed brain-wide concordance using whole-brain parcellation. Results demonstrated widespread cross-brain synchrony in both the PCN and across the neuroaxis, from primary sensory/somatosensory areas, through insular-cingulate regions, to temporal and prefrontal cortices. The Social context yielded significantly more cross-brain concordance, with PCNs striatum, parahippocampal gyrus, superior temporal sulcus, ACC, and PFC displaying cross-brain synchrony only to mother-infant social cues. Moment-by-moment fluctuations in mother-infant social synchrony, ranging from episodes of low synchrony to tightly coordinated positive bouts, were tracked online by cross-brain concordance in the preregistered ACC. Findings indicate that social attachment stimuli, representing evolutionary-salient universal cues that require no verbal narrative, trigger substantial interbrain concordance and suggest that the mother-infant bond, an icon standing at the heart of human civilization, may function to glue brains into a unified experience and bind humans into social groups.

Significance statement: Infant stimuli elicit widespread neural response in human adults, attesting to their evolutionary significance, but do they also trigger cross-brain concordance and induce neural uniformity among perceivers? We measured cross-brain synchrony to ecological mother-infant videos. We used theory-driven analysis, measuring cross-brain concordance in the parenting network, and data-driven analysis, assessing brain-wide concordance using whole-brain parcellation. Attachment cues triggered widespread cross-brain concordance in both the parenting network and across the neuroaxis. Moment-by-moment fluctuations in behavioral synchrony were tracked online by cross-brain variability in ACC. Attachment reminders bind humans' brains into a unitary experience and stimuli characterized by social synchrony enhance neural similarity among participants, describing one mechanism by which attachment bonds provide the neural template for the consolidation of social groups.

Early-life digital media experiences and development of atypical sensory processing

Heffler, K. F., Acharya, B., Subedi, K., & Bennett, D. S. (2024). Early-life digital media experiences and development of atypical sensory processing. *JAMA Pediatrics, 178*(3), 266–273. doi:10.1001/jamapediatrics.2023.5923

Abstract

Importance: Atypical sensory processing is challenging for children and families, yet there is limited understanding of its associated risk factors.

Objective: To determine the association between early-life digital media exposure and sensory processing outcomes among toddlers.

Design, setting, and participants: This multicenter US study used data that were analyzed from the National Children's Study (NCS), a cohort study of environmental influences on child health and development, with enrollment from 2011 to 2014. Data analysis was performed in 2023. The study included children enrolled in the NCS at birth whose caregivers completed reports of digital media exposure and sensory processing.

Exposures: Children's viewing of television or video at 12 months (yes or no), 18 months, and 24 months of age (hours per day).

Main outcomes and measures: Sensory processing was reported at approximately 33 months of age on the Infant/Toddler Sensory Profile. Quadrant scores (low registration, sensation seeking, sensory sensitivity, and sensation avoiding) were categorized into groups representing typical, high, and low sensory-related behaviors, and multinomial regression analyses were performed.

Results: A total of 1,471 children (50% male) were included. Screen exposure at 12 months of age was associated with two-fold increased odds of being in the high category of low registration (odds ratio [OR], 2.05; 95% CI, 1.31–3.20), while the odds of being in the low category instead of the typical category decreased for sensation seeking (OR, 0.55; 95% CI, 0.35–0.87), sensation avoiding (OR, 0.69; 95% CI, 0.50–0.94), and low registration (OR, 0.64; 95% CI, 0.44–0.92). At 18 months of age, greater screen exposure was associated with increased risk of high sensation avoiding (OR, 1.23; 95% CI, 1.03–1.46) and low registration (OR, 1.23; 95% CI, 1.04–1.44). At 24 months of age, greater screen exposure was associated with increased risk of high sensation seeking (OR, 1.20; 95% CI, 1.02–1.42), sensory sensitivity (OR, 1.25; 95% CI, 1.05–1.49), and sensation avoiding (OR, 1.21; 95% CI, 1.03–1.42).

Conclusions and relevance: In this cohort study, early-life digital media exposure was associated with atypical sensory processing outcomes in multiple domains. These findings suggest that digital media exposure might be a potential risk factor for the development of atypical sensory profiles. Further research is needed to understand the relationship between screen time and specific sensory-related developmental and behavioral outcomes, and whether minimizing early-life exposure can improve subsequent sensory-related outcomes.

Mothers and fathers show different neural synchrony with their children during shared experiences

Liu, Q., Zhu, S., Zhou, X., Liu, F., Becker, B., Kendrick, K. M., & Zhao, W. (2024). Mothers and fathers show different neural synchrony with their children during shared experiences. *NeuroImage, 288*, 120529. doi:10.1016/j.neuroimage.2024.120529

Abstract

Parent-child shared experiences have an important influence on social development in children, although contributions of mothers and fathers may differ. Neural synchronicity occurs between mothers and fathers and their children during social interactions, but it is unclear whether they differ in this respect. We used data from simultaneous fNIRS hyperscanning in mothers (n = 33) and fathers (n = 29) and their children (3–4 years) to determine different patterns and strengths of neural synchronization in the frontal cortex during co-viewing of videos or free-play.

Mothers showed greater synchrony with child than fathers during passive viewing of videos and the synchronization was positively associated with video complexity and negatively associated with parental stress. During play interactions, mothers showed more controlling behaviors over their child and greater evidence for joint gaze and joint imitation play with child whereas fathers spent more time gazing at other things. In addition, different aspects of child communication promoted neural synchrony between mothers and fathers and child during active play interactions. Overall, our findings indicate greater neural and behavioral synchrony between mothers than fathers and young children during passive or active shared experiences, although for both it was weakened by parental distress and child difficulty.

When do children begin to care for others? The ontogenetic growth of empathic concern across the first two years of life

Paulus, M., Becher, T., Christner, N., Kammermeier, M., Gniewosz, B., & Pletti, C. (2024). When do children begin to care for others? The ontogenetic growth of empathic concern across the first two years of life. *Cognitive Development, 70*, 101439. doi:10.1016/j.cogdev.2024.101439

Abstract

Empathic concern for others plays a central role for human cooperation and is proposed to be key in moral development. Developmental theories disagree on the age of emergence of empathic concern in human ontogeny and the factors supporting its early development. To assess different theoretical views, the current study longitudinally assessed infants' (N = 127) reactions towards an experimenter and their mothers simulating pain at 6, 10, 14, and 18 months. As an emotional control condition, infants' reactions towards a laughing experimenter were assessed. Maternal sensitivity, children's temperamental emotionality, and self-recognition were included as predictors. True intraindividual change models were applied to capture the growth of empathic concern in early development. Overall, there were minor and inconsistent differences in children's responses to laughing and crying others in the first year of life, whereas clear differences emerged in the second year. At 6 months, scale values of empathic concern were significantly related to measures of infant distress suggesting that infants experience emotional contagion and not veridical empathic concern. At 18 months, children's concern towards the experimenter was related to their concern towards their mother. Maternal sensitivity, negative emotionality, and self-recognition were related to children's empathic concern within the second year. These findings suggest that empathic concern emerges in the second year and point to a gradual emergence of concern for others in human ontogeny.

ENVIRONMENT

Immersion in nature enhances neural indices of executive attention

McDonnell, A. S., & Strayer, D. L. (2024). Immersion in nature enhances neural indices of executive attention. *Scientific Reports, 14*(1), 1845. doi:10.1038/s41598-024-52205-1

Abstract

There is conjecture that our modern urban environments place high demand on our attentional resources, which can become depleted over time and cause mental fatigue. Natural environments, on the other hand, are thought to provide relief from this demand and allow our resources to be replenished. While these claims have been assessed with self-report and behavioral measures, there is limited understanding of the neural mechanisms underlying these attentional benefits. The present randomized controlled trial fills this gap in the literature by using electroencephalography to explore three aspects of attention—alerting, orienting, and executive control—from a behavioral and neural perspective. Participants (N = 92) completed the Attention Network Task before and after either a 40-minute walk in nature or a 40-minute walk in a control, urban environment. Participants that walked in nature reported their walk to be more restorative than those that walked in the urban environment. Furthermore, the nature group showed an enhanced error-related negativity after their walk, an event-related brain component that indexes executive control capacity, whereas the urban group did not. These findings demonstrate that a 40-minute nature walk enhances executive control at a neural level, providing a potential neural mechanism for attention restoration in nature.

Mechanisms underlying the associations between different types of nature exposure and sleep duration: An 18-country analysis

Martin, L., White, M. P., Elliott, L. R., Grellier, J., Astell-Burt, T., Bratman, G. N., … Fleming, L. E. (2024). Mechanisms underlying the associations between different types of nature exposure and sleep duration: An 18-country analysis. *Environmental Research, 250*, 118522. doi:10.1016/j.envres.2024.118522

Abstract
While green space has been linked to healthier sleep outcomes, the roles of specific types of nature exposure, potential underlying mechanisms, and between-country variations in nature-sleep associations have received little attention. Drawing on cross-sectional survey data from an 18-country sample of adults (N = 16,077) the current study examined: (a) the relative associations between six different types of nature exposure (streetscape greenery, blue view from home, green space within 1 km, coast within 1 km, green space visits, blue space visits) and insufficient sleep (<6 h vs. 7–10 h per day); (b) whether these relationships were mediated by better mental wellbeing and/or physical activity; and (c) the consistency of these pathways among the different countries. After controlling for covariates, neighborhood nature measures (green space, coast within 1 km) were not significantly associated with insufficient sleep; but nature visible from home (streetscape greenery, blue views) and recreational visits to green and blue spaces were each associated with less insufficient sleep. Significant nature-sleep associations were mediated, to varying degrees, by better mental wellbeing but not self-reported physical activity. Country-level heterogeneity in the strength of nature-sleep associations was observed. Increasing nature visible from the home may represent a promising strategy for promoting healthier sleep duration at the population level, while nature-based interventions encouraging individuals to spend time in local green/blue spaces may be an appropriate target to assist individuals affected by insufficient sleep.

Urban green and blue spaces and general and mental health among older adults in Washington state: Analysis of BRFSS data between 2011–2019

Vegaraju, A., & Amiri, S. (2024). Urban green and blue spaces and general and mental health among older adults in Washington state: Analysis of BRFSS data between 2011–2019. *Health and Place, 85*, 103148. doi:10.1016/j.healthplace.2023.103148

Abstract
A growing body of evidence highlights the significant effect of built environment features on mental and general health. This study examined the association between distance to and percentage of green and blue space measures and serious psychological distress, general health, and frequent mental distress among older adults living in urban ZIP codes in Washington state. Percentage of green space, particularly tree canopy and forest space, was significantly associated with better self-rated general health and reduced odds of serious psychological distress. Closer distance to blue space was associated with better self-rated general health. Programs that incentivize exposure to green and blue spaces for urban-dwelling, older adults may improve health outcomes.

Prenatal exposure to ambient $PM_{2.5}$ and its chemical constituents and child intelligence quotient at 6 years of age

Sun, X., Liu, C., Ji, H., Li, W., Miao, M., Yuan, W., … Kan, H. (2023). Prenatal exposure to ambient $PM_{2.5}$ and its chemical constituents and child intelligence quotient at 6 years of age. *Ecotoxicology and Environmental Safety, 255*, 114813. doi:10.1016/j.ecoenv.2023.114813

Abstract
There are limited studies on the associations between prenatal exposure to constituents of fine particulate matter ($PM_{2.5}$) and children's intelligence quotient (IQ). Our study aimed to explore the associations between prenatal $PM_{2.5}$ and its six constituents and the IQ levels of 6-year-old children. We included 512 mother-child pairs. We used a satellite-based modeling framework to estimate prenatal $PM_{2.5}$ and its six constituents (ammonium, sulfate, nitrate, organic carbon, soil dust, and black carbon). We assessed the children's IQ using the short form of

the Wechsler Intelligence Scale. Perceptual Reasoning Index (PRI), Verbal Comprehension Index (VCI), and Full Scale IQ (FSIQ) scores were computed. The multiple informant model (MIM) was applied to explore the trimester specific effects of $PM_{2.5}$ and its six constituents' exposure on children's PRI, VCI, and FSIQ. To examine whether the duration of breastfeeding and physical activity (PA) could modify the effects of $PM_{2.5}$ on children's IQ, we stratified the analyses according to the duration of breastfeeding (≤6 and >6 months) and time of outdoor activities after school (≤2 and >2 h/week). The first trimester $PM_{2.5}$ and its five constituents' exposures were inversely associated with FSIQ ($\beta = -1.34$, 95% confidence interval [CI] [–2.71, 0.04] for $PM_{2.5}$) and PRI ($\beta = -2.18$, 95% CI [–3.80, –0.57] for $PM_{2.5}$) in children. The associations were magnified among boys and those with less outdoor activities or shorter breastfeeding duration. Our results indicate that prenatal $PM_{2.5}$ and several of its main constituents' exposure may disrupt cognitive development in children aged 6 years. More PA and longer breastfeeding duration may alleviate the detrimental effects of prenatal $PM_{2.5}$ exposure on children's cognitive function.

GENES

Gene expression networks regulated by human personality

Del Val, C., Díaz de la Guardia-Bolívar, E., Zwir, I., Mishra, P. P., Mesa, A., Salas, R., … Cloninger, C. R. (2024). Gene expression networks regulated by human personality. *Molecular Psychiatry*, 1–20. doi:10.1038/s41380-024-02484-x

Abstract

Genome-wide association studies of human personality have been carried out, but transcription of the whole genome has not been studied in relation to personality in humans. We collected genome-wide expression profiles of adults to characterize the regulation of expression and function in genes related to human personality. We devised an innovative multi-omic approach to network analysis to identify the key control elements and interactions in multi-modular networks. We identified sets of transcribed genes that were co-expressed in specific brain regions with genes known to be associated with personality. Then we identified the minimum networks for the co-localized genes using bioinformatic resources. Subjects were 459 adults from the Young Finns Study who completed the Temperament and Character Inventory and provided peripheral blood for genomic and transcriptomic analysis. We identified an extrinsic network of 45 regulatory genes from seed genes in brain regions involved in self-regulation of emotional reactivity to extracellular stimuli (e.g., self-regulation of anxiety) and an intrinsic network of 43 regulatory genes from seed genes in brain regions involved in self-regulation of interpretations of meaning (e.g., production of concepts and language). We discovered that interactions between the two networks were coordinated by a control hub of three miRNAs and three protein-coding genes shared by both. Interactions of the control hub with proteins and ncRNAs identified more than 100 genes that overlap directly with known personality-related genes and more than another 4,000 genes that interact indirectly. We conclude that the six-gene hub is the crux of an integrative network that orchestrates information-transfer throughout a multi-modular system of over 4000 genes enriched in liquid-liquid-phase-separation (LLPS)–related RNAs, diverse transcription factors, and hominid-specific miRNAs and lncRNAs. Gene expression networks associated with human personality regulate neuronal plasticity, epigenesis, and adaptive functioning by the interactions of salience and meaning in self-awareness.

PAIN

Reattribution to mind-brain processes and recovery from chronic back pain: A secondary analysis of a randomized clinical trial

Ashar, Y. K., Lumley, M. A., Perlis, R. H., Liston, C., Gunning, F. M., & Wager, T. D. (2023). Reattribution to mind-brain processes and recovery from chronic back pain: A secondary analysis of a randomized clinical trial. *JAMA Network Open, 6*(9), e2333846–e2333846. doi:10.1001/jamanetworkopen.2023.33846

Abstract

Importance: In primary chronic back pain (CBP), the belief that pain indicates tissue damage is both inaccurate and unhelpful. Reattributing pain to mind or brain processes may support recovery.

Objectives: To test whether the reattribution of pain to mind or brain processes was associated with pain relief in pain reprocessing therapy (PRT) and to validate natural language-based tools for measuring patients' symptom attributions.

Design, setting, and participants: This secondary analysis of clinical trial data analyzed natural language data from patients with primary CBP randomized to PRT, placebo injection control, or usual care control groups and treated in a US university research setting. Eligible participants were adults aged 21 to 70 years with CBP recruited from the community. Enrollment extended from 2017 to 2018, with the current analyses conducted from 2020 to 2022.

Interventions: PRT included cognitive, behavioral, and somatic techniques to support reattributing pain to non-dangerous, reversible mind or brain causes. Subcutaneous placebo injection and usual care were hypothesized not to affect pain attributions.

Main outcomes and measures: At pretreatment and posttreatment, participants listed their top three perceived causes of pain in their own words (e.g., football injury, bad posture, stress); pain intensity was measured as last-week average pain (0 to 10 rating, with 0 indicating no pain and 10 indicating greatest pain). The number of attributions categorized by masked coders as reflecting mind or brain processes were summed to yield mind-brain attribution scores (range, 0–3). An automated scoring algorithm was developed and benchmarked against human coder-derived scores. A data-driven natural language processing (NLP) algorithm identified the dimensional structure of pain attributions.

Results: We enrolled 151 adults (81 female [54%], 134 White [89%], mean [*SD*] age, 41.1 [15.6] years) reporting moderate severity CBP (mean [*SD*] intensity, 4.10 [1.26]; mean [*SD*] duration, 10.0 [8.9] years). At pretreatment, 41 attributions (10%) were categorized as mind- or brain-related across intervention conditions. PRT led to significant increases in mind- or brain-related attributions, with 71 posttreatment attributions (51%) in the PRT condition categorized as mind- or brain-related, as compared with 22 (8%) in control conditions (mind-brain attribution scores: PRT vs. placebo, $g = 1.95$ [95% CI, 1.45–2.47]; PRT vs. usual care, $g = 2.06$ [95% CI, 1.57–2.60]). Consistent with hypothesized PRT mechanisms, increases in mind-brain attribution score were associated with reductions in pain intensity at posttreatment (standardized $\beta = -0.25$; $t127 = -2.06$; $p = .04$) and mediated the effects of PRT vs. control on 1-year follow-up pain intensity ($\beta = -0.35$ [95% CI, –0.07 to –0.63]; $p = .05$). The automated word-counting algorithm and human coder-derived scores achieved moderate and substantial agreement at pretreatment and posttreatment (Cohen $\kappa = 0.42$ and 0.68, respectively). The data-driven NLP algorithm identified a principal dimension of mind and brain vs. biomechanical attributions, converging with hypothesis-driven analyses.

Conclusions and relevance: In this secondary analysis of a randomized trial, PRT increased attribution of primary CBP to mind- or brain-related causes. Increased mind-brain attribution was associated with reductions in pain intensity.

PTSD/TRAUMA

Adverse childhood experiences and adult mental health outcomes

Daníelsdóttir, H. B., Aspelund, T., Shen, Q., Halldorsdottir, T., Jakobsdóttir, J., Song, H., … Valdimarsdóttir, U. A. (2024). Adverse childhood experiences and adult mental health outcomes. *JAMA Psychiatry*, e240039. doi:10.1001/jamapsychiatry.2024.0039

Abstract

Importance: Exposure to adverse childhood experiences (ACEs) has consistently been associated with multiple negative mental health outcomes extending into adulthood. However, given that ACEs and psychiatric disorders cluster within families, it remains to be comprehensively assessed to what extent familial confounding contributes to associations between ACEs and clinically confirmed adult psychiatric disorders.

Objective: To investigate whether associations between ACEs and adult mental health outcomes remain after adjusting for familial (genetic and environmental) confounding.

Design, setting, and participants: This Swedish twin cohort study used a discordant twin pair design based on monozygotic (MZ) and dizygotic (DZ) twins. A total of 25 252 adult twins (aged 18–47 years) from the Swedish Twin Registry born between 1959 and 1998 were followed up from age 19 years until 2016, with a maximum follow-up time of 39 years. Data were analyzed from April 2022 to November 2023.

Exposures: A total of 7 ACEs, including family violence, emotional abuse or neglect, physical neglect, physical abuse, sexual abuse, rape, and hate crime, were assessed with items from the Life Stressor Checklist–Revised in a web-based survey.

Main outcomes and measures: Adult (ages >18 years) clinical diagnosis of psychiatric disorders (i.e., depressive, anxiety, alcohol or drug misuse, or stress-related disorders) were obtained from the Swedish National Patient Register.

Results: Of 25,252 twins included in the study (15,038 female [59.6%]; mean [*SD*] age at ACE assessment, 29.9 [8.7] years), 9,751 individuals (38.6%) reported exposure to at least 1 ACE. A greater number of ACEs was associated with increased odds of any psychiatric disorder in the full cohort (odds ratio [OR] per additional ACE, 1.52; 95% CI, 1.48–1.57). The association remained but ORs per additional ACE were attenuated in DZ (1.29; 95% CI, 1.14–1.47) and MZ (1.20; 95% CI, 1.02–1.40) twin pairs. Individuals who were exposed to sexual abuse compared with those who were not exposed had increased odds of any clinically confirmed psychiatric disorder in all comparisons: full cohort (OR, 3.09; 95% CI, 2.68–3.56), DZ twin pairs (OR, 2.10; 95% CI, 1.33–3.32), and MZ twin pairs (1.80; 95% CI, 1.04–3.11).

Conclusions and relevance: This study found that associations between ACEs and adult mental health outcomes remained after controlling for shared genetic and environmental factors, which was particularly evident after multiple ACEs or sexual abuse. These findings suggest that targeted interventions may be associated with reduced risks of future psychopathology.

OTHER HEALTH ISSUES

Racism and health: Evidence and needed research

Williams, D. R., Lawrence, J. A., & Davis, B. A. (2019). Racism and health: Evidence and needed research. *Annual Review of Public Health, 40*, 105–125. doi:10.1146/annurev-publhealth-040218-043750

Abstract

In recent decades, there has been remarkable growth in scientific research examining the multiple ways in which racism can adversely affect health. This interest has been driven in part by the striking persistence of racial/ethnic inequities in health and the empirical evidence that indicates that socioeconomic factors alone do not account for racial/ethnic inequities in health. Racism is considered a fundamental cause of adverse health outcomes for racial/ethnic minorities and racial/ethnic inequities in health. This article provides an overview of the evidence linking the primary domains of racism—structural racism, cultural racism, and individual-level discrimination—to mental and physical health outcomes. For each mechanism, we describe key findings and identify priorities for future research. We also discuss evidence for interventions to reduce racism and describe research needed to advance knowledge in this area.

Relationship between severe mental illness and physical multimorbidity: A meta-analysis and call for action

Pizzol, D., Trott, M., Butler, L., Barnett, Y., Ford, T., Neufeld, S. A., … Smith, L. (2023). Relationship between severe mental illness and physical multimorbidity: A meta-analysis and call for action. *BMJ Mental Health, 26*(1), e300870. doi:10.1136/bmjment-2023-300870

Abstract

Background: People with severe mental illness (SMI) have a higher prevalence of several chronic physical health conditions, and the prevalence of physical multimorbidity is expected to rise. The aim of this study was to assess the strength of the association between SMI and physical multimorbidity.

Study selection and analysis: We systematically searched PubMed/Medline, Scopus, Embase, Web of Science, PsycINFO, and the behavioral sciences collection databases, from inception to 31 January 2023, for studies that investigated the association between SMI and physical multimorbidity. Humans of any age either clinically diagnosed and/or currently receiving treatment for SMI, specified as schizophrenia (and related psychotic disorders), bipolar disorder, and psychotic depression, were eligible. Data from studies selected for inclusion were converted into ORs, with a subsequent meta-analysis conducted.

Findings: We included 19 studies with a total of 194,123 patients with SMI with different diagnoses and drawn from the general population. The pooled OR for physical multimorbidity in people with versus without SMI was 1.84 (95% CI 1.33 to 2.54), with the analysis indicating a high level of heterogeneity (98.38%). The other 15 studies included in the systematic review for which it was not possible to conduct a meta-analysis showed strong associations between SMI and physical multimorbidity.

Conclusions: The current evidence highlights the link between SMI and physical multimorbidity. A multidisciplinary approach is now urgent to develop the best models of services tailored to patients with SMI with physical multimorbidities to improve physical, mental, and social outcomes.

The social media diet: A scoping review to investigate the association between social media, body image and eating disorders amongst young people

Dane, A., & Bhatia, K. (2023). The social media diet: A scoping review to investigate the association between social media, body image and eating disorders amongst young people. *PLOS Global Public Health, 3*(3), e0001091. doi:10.1371/journal.pgph.0001091

Abstract

Background: Eating disorders are a group of heterogenous, disabling, and deadly psychiatric illnesses with a plethora of associated health consequences. Exploratory research suggests that social media usage may be triggering body image concerns and heightening eating disorder pathology amongst young people, but the topic is underresearched as a global public health issue.

Aim: To systematically map out and critically review the existing global literature on the relationship between social media usage, body image, and eating disorders in young people aged 10–24 years.

Methods: A systematic search of MEDLINE, PyscINFO, and Web of Science for research on social media use and body image concerns/disordered eating outcomes published between January 2016 and July 2021. Results on exposures (social media usage), outcomes (body image, eating disorders, disordered eating), mediators, and moderators were synthesized using an integrated theoretical framework of the influence of internet use on body image concerns and eating pathology.

Results: Evidence from 50 studies in 17 countries indicates that social media usage leads to body image concerns, eating disorders/disordered eating, and poor mental health via the mediating pathways of social comparison, thin/fit ideal internalization, and self-objectification. Specific exposures (social media trends, pro-eating disorder content, appearance focused platforms, and investment in photos) and moderators (high BMI, female gender, and pre-existing body image concerns) strengthen the relationship, while other moderators (high social media literacy and body appreciation) are protective, hinting at a "self-perpetuating cycle of risk."

Conclusion: Social media usage is a plausible risk factor for the development of eating disorders. Research from Asia suggests that the association is not unique to traditionally western cultures. Based on the scale of social media usage amongst young people, this issue is worthy of attention as an emerging global public health issue.

Can inflammation predict social media use? Linking a biological marker of systemic inflammation with social media use among college students and middle-aged adults

Lee, D. S., Jiang, T., Crocker, J., & Way, B. M. (2023). Can inflammation predict social media use? Linking a biological marker of systemic inflammation with social media use among college students and middle-aged adults. *Brain, Behavior, and Immunity, 112*, 1–10. doi:10.1016/j.bbi.2023.05.010

Abstract

Drawing on recent evidence that inflammation may promote social affiliative motivation, the present research proposes a novel perspective that inflammation may be associated with more social media use. In a cross-sectional analysis of a nationally representative sample, Study 1 ($N = 863$) found a positive association between C-reactive protein (CRP), a biomarker of systemic inflammation, and the amount of social media use by middle-aged adults. Study 2 ($N = 228$) showed that among college students CRP was prospectively associated with more social media use 6 weeks later. Providing stronger evidence of the directionality of this effect, Study 3 ($N = 171$) showed that in college students CRP predicted increased social media use in the subsequent week even after controlling for current week's use. Additionally, in exploratory analyses of CRP and different types of social media use in the same week, CRP was only associated with using social media for social interaction and not for other purposes (e.g., entertainment). The present research sheds light on the social effects of inflammation and highlights potential benefits of using social media as a context for studying the impact of inflammation on social motivation and behavior.

Feelings in words: Emotion word use and cardiovascular reactivity in marital interactions

Meier, T., Stephens, J. E., & Haase, C. M. (2023). Feelings in words: Emotion word use and cardiovascular reactivity in marital interactions. *Emotion, 24*(3), 733–744. doi:10.1037/emo0001299

Abstract

Putting feelings into words is often thought to be beneficial. Few studies, however, have examined associations between natural emotion word use and cardiovascular reactivity. This laboratory-based study examined emotion word use (i.e., from computerized text analysis) and cardiovascular reactivity (i.e., interbeat interval changes from baseline) across two interaction contexts (i.e., conflict and positive conversations) in 49 mixed-sex married couples (age: $M = 43.11$, $SD = 9.20$) from diverse socioeconomic backgrounds. We focused on both frequency (i.e., relative proportion of emotion words) and diversity (i.e., relative proportion of unique emotion words) of emotion words. Data were collected between 2015 and 2017 and analyzed treating both partners and conversations as repeated measures, resulting in 196 observations overall (four per dyad). Findings showed that (a) when spouses used more negative emotion words (especially anger), they showed higher cardiovascular reactivity. This finding was robust when controlling for covariates; generalized across gender, interaction contexts, and socioeconomic status. Moreover, (b) when spouses used a more diverse negative emotion vocabulary, they showed higher cardiovascular reactivity, but this was not robust when controlling for negative emotion word frequency. Associations between (c) positive emotion word use and cardiovascular reactivity were not statistically significant. Verbalizing negative emotions thus seems to go along with higher cardiovascular reactivity, at least in the short term. Replication is needed across other relationship types, genders, and sexual orientations. These findings highlight emotion word use as an indicator of cardiovascular reactivity, which has implications for the identification of potential health risks that emerge during marital interactions.

Association of cannabis use with cardiovascular outcomes among US adults

Jeffers, A. M., Glantz, S., Byers, A. L., & Keyhani, S. (2024). Association of cannabis use with cardiovascular outcomes among US adults. *Journal of the American Heart Association, 3*(5), e030178. doi:10.1161/JAHA.123.030178

Abstract

Background: We examined the association between cannabis use and cardiovascular outcomes among the general population, among never-tobacco smokers, and among younger individuals.

Methods and results: This is a population-based, cross-sectional study of 2016 to 2020 data from the Behavioral Risk Factor Surveillance Survey from 27 American states and 2 territories. We assessed the association of cannabis use (number of days of cannabis use in the past 30 days) with self-reported cardiovascular outcomes (coronary heart disease, myocardial infarction, stroke, and a composite measure of all three) in multivariable regression models, adjusting for tobacco use and other characteristics in adults 18 to 74 years old. We repeated this analysis among nontobacco smokers, and among men <55 years old and women <65 years old who are at risk of premature cardiovascular disease. Among the 434,104 respondents, the prevalence of daily and nondaily cannabis use was 4% and 7.1%, respectively. The adjusted odds ratio (aOR) for the association of daily cannabis use and coronary heart disease, myocardial infarction, stroke, and the composite outcome (coronary heart disease, myocardial infarction, and stroke) was 1.16 (95% CI, 0.98–1.38), 1.25 (95% CI, 1.07–1.46), 1.42 (95% CI, 1.20–1.68), and 1.28 (95% CI, 1.13–1.44), respectively, with proportionally lower log odds for days of use between 0 and 30 days per month. Among never-tobacco smokers, daily cannabis use was also associated with myocardial infarction (aOR, 1.49 [95% CI, 1.03–2.15]), stroke (aOR, 2.16 [95% CI, 1.43–3.25]), and the composite of coronary heart disease, myocardial infarction, and stroke (aOR, 1.77 [95% CI, 1.31–2.40]). Relationships between cannabis use and cardiovascular outcomes were similar for men <55 years old and women <65 years old.

Conclusions: Cannabis use is associated with adverse cardiovascular outcomes, with heavier use (more days per month) associated with higher odds of adverse outcomes.

Prospective associations of accelerometer-measured machine-learned sedentary behavior with death among older women: The OPACH study

Nguyen, S., Bellettiere, J., Anuskiewicz, B., Di, C., Carlson, J., Natarajan, L., … LaCroix, A. Z. (2024). Prospective associations of accelerometer-measured machine-learned sedentary behavior with death among older women: The OPACH study. *Journal of the American Heart Association*, e031156. doi:10.1161/JAHA.123.031156

Abstract

Background: Sedentary behavior is a recognized mortality risk factor. The novel and validated convolutional neural network hip accelerometer posture algorithm highly accurately classifies sitting and postural changes compared with accelerometer count cut points. We examined the prospective associations of convolutional neural network hip accelerometer posture-classified total sitting time and mean sitting bout duration with all-cause and cardiovascular disease (CVD) death.

Methods and results: Women ($n = 5856$; mean ± *SD* age, 79±7 years; 33% Black women, 17% Hispanic or Latina women, 50% White women) in the Women's Health Initiative Objective Physical Activity and Cardiovascular Health (OPACH) study wore the ActiGraph GT3X+ for ~7 days from May 2012 to April 2014 and were followed through February 19, 2022 for all-cause and CVD death. The convolutional neural network hip accelerometer posture algorithm classified total sitting time and mean sitting bout duration from GT3X+ output. Over follow-up (median, 8.4 years; range, 0.1–9.9), there were 1,733 deaths (632 from CVD). Adjusted Cox regression hazard ratios (HRs) comparing women in the highest total sitting time quartile (>696 min/d) to those in the lowest (<556.0 min/d) were 1.57 (95% CI; 1.35–1.83; *p*-trend<0.001) for all-cause death and 1.78 (95% CI; 1.36–2.31; *p*-trend<0.001) for CVD death. HRs comparing women in the longest mean sitting bout duration quartile (>15 minutes) to the shortest (<9.3 minutes) were 1.43 (95% CI; 1.23–1.66; *p*-trend<0.001) for all-cause death and 1.52 (95% CI; 1.18–1.96; *p*-trend<0.001) for CVD death. Apparent nonlinear associations for total sitting time suggested higher all-cause death (*p* nonlinear = 0.009) and CVD death (P nonlinear = 0.008) risk after ~660 to 700 min/d.

Conclusions: Higher total sitting time and longer mean sitting bout duration are associated with higher all-cause and CVD mortality risk among older women. These data support interventions aimed at reducing both total sitting time and interrupting prolonged sitting.

STRESS

Effects of a digital mental health intervention on perceived stress and rumination in adolescents aged 13 to 17 years: Randomized controlled trial

Boucher, E. M., Ward, H., Miles, C. J., Henry, R. D., & Stoeckl, S. E. (2024). Effects of a digital mental health intervention on perceived stress and rumination in adolescents aged 13 to 17 years: Randomized controlled trial. *Journal of Medical Internet Research, 26*, e54282. doi:10.2196/54282

Abstract

Background: Although adolescents report high levels of stress, they report engaging in few stress management techniques. Consequently, developing effective and targeted programs to help address this transdiagnostic risk factor in adolescence is particularly important. Most stress management programs for adolescents are delivered within schools, and the evidence for these programs is mixed, suggesting a need for alternative options for stress management among adolescents.

Objective: The aim of the study is to test the short-term effects of a self-guided digital mental health intervention (DMHI) designed for adolescents on perceived stress and rumination (i.e., brooding).

Methods: This was a 12-week, 2-arm decentralized randomized controlled trial of adolescents aged 13 to 17 years who presented with elevated levels of perceived stress and brooding. Participants were randomly assigned to engage with a self-guided DMHI (Happify for Teens) or to a waitlist control. Participants assigned to the intervention group were given access to the program for 12 weeks. Happify for Teens consists of various evidence-based activities drawn from therapeutic modalities such as cognitive behavioral therapy, positive psychology, and mindfulness, which are then organized into several programs targeting specific areas of concern (e.g., Stress Buster 101). Participants in the waitlist control received access to this product for 12 weeks upon completing the study. Participants in both groups completed measures of perceived stress, brooding, optimism, sleep disturbance, and loneliness at baseline, 4 weeks, 8 weeks, and 12 weeks. Changes in outcomes between the intervention and waitlist control groups were assessed using repeated-measures multilevel models.

Results: Of the 303 participants included in data analyses, 132 were assigned to the intervention and 171 to the waitlist. There were significantly greater improvements in the intervention condition for perceived stress (intervention: $b = -1.50$; 95% CI −1.82 to −1.19; $p < .001$ and control: $b = -0.09$; 95% CI −0.44 to 0.26; $p = .61$), brooding (intervention: $b = -0.84$; 95% CI −1.00 to −0.68; $p < .001$ and control: $b = -0.30$; 95% CI −0.47 to −0.12; $p = .001$), and loneliness (intervention: $b = -0.96$; 95% CI −1.2 to −0.73; $p < .001$ and control: $b = -0.38$; 95% CI: −0.64 to −0.12; $p = .005$) over the 12-week study period. Changes in optimism and sleep disturbance were not significantly different across groups ($ps \geq .096$).

Conclusions: Happify for Teens was effective at reducing perceived stress, rumination, and loneliness among adolescents over 12 weeks when compared to a waitlist control group. Our data reveal the potential benefits of DMHIs for adolescents, which may present a more scalable, destigmatized, and cost-effective alternative to school-based programs.

The power of human touch: Physical contact improves performance in basketball free throws

Büttner, C. M., Kenntemich, C., & Williams, K. D. (2024). The power of human touch: Physical contact improves performance in basketball free throws. *Psychology of Sport and Exercise, 72*, 102610. doi:10.1016/j.psychsport.2024.102610

Abstract

How pervasive is the power of human touch? Physical touch by other humans shows social support and alleviates stress—stress that may otherwise interfere with performance in athletic tasks. We argue that physical touch improves performance in highly stressful situations: free throws in basketball. In two studies (*N*total = 60 NCAAW games, *k*total = 835 free throw tandems), we assessed how often teammates touched the shooting player (e.g., a tap on the shoulder) in between shooting two free throws. We find that the extent of touch (i.e., being touched by 0, 1, 2, 3, or all 4 teammates) after the first free throw predicted success with the second free throw, but only when players missed the first free throw (integrated data analysis: main effect hand taps: $b = 0.47, p = .021$; main effect first free throw: $b = 1.36, p = .019$; interaction effect: $b = -0.55, p = .024$). We argue that this means that teammates' support expressed in physical touch helps particularly when stress levels are already high. Results are robust when controlling for players' skill level, home versus away games, point difference, and remaining playing time. More frequent touch was also tendentially associated with teams' season success (ACC-teams only, main effect of hand taps: $b = -0.42, p = .062$). Physical touch thus indeed boosts performance under stress, superseding a range of other factors, likely also in other team sports and interpersonal relationships.

WELLBEING

A meta-analytic review of anger management activities that increase or decrease arousal: What fuels or douses rage?

Kjærvik, S. L., & Bushman, B. J. (2024). A meta-analytic review of anger management activities that increase or decrease arousal: What fuels or douses rage? *Clinical Psychology Review, 109*, 102414. doi:10.1016/j.cpr.2024.102414

Abstract

Anger is an unpleasant emotion that most people want to get rid of. Some anger management activities focus on decreasing arousal (e.g., deep breathing, mindfulness, meditation), whereas others focus on increasing arousal (e.g., hitting a bag, jogging, cycling). This meta-analytic review, based on 154 studies including 184 independent samples involving 10,189 participants, tested the effectiveness of both types of activities. The results indicated that arousal-decreasing activities decreased anger and aggression ($g = -0.63$, [–0.82, –0.43]), and the results were robust. Effects were stable over time for participants of different genders, races, ages, and cultures. Arousal-decreasing activities were effective in students and non-students, in criminal offenders and non-offenders, and in individuals with and without intellectual disabilities. Arousal-decreasing activities were effective regardless of how they were delivered (e.g., digital platforms, researchers, therapists), in both group and individual sessions, and in both field and laboratory settings. In contrast, arousal-increasing activities were ineffective overall ($g = -0.02$, [–0.13, 0.09]) and were heterogenous and complex. These findings do not support the ideas that venting anger or going for a run are effective anger management activities. A more effective approach for managing anger is "turning down the heat" or calming down by engaging in activities that decrease arousal.

Trajectories of digital flourishing in adolescence: The predictive roles of developmental changes and digital divide factors

Rosič, J., Schreurs, L., Janicke-Bowles, S. H., & Vandenbosch, L. (2024). Trajectories of digital flourishing in adolescence: The predictive roles of developmental changes and digital divide factors. *Child Development*. doi:10.1111/cdev.1410

Abstract

Digital flourishing refers to the positive perceptions of digital communication use in five dimensions: connectedness, positive social comparison, authentic self-presentation, civil participation, and self-control. This three-wave panel study among 1,081 Slovenian adolescents (*M* age = 15.34 years, 53.8% boys, 80.7% ethnic majority) explored the trajectories of their digital flourishing dimensions over 1 year (2021–2022). Latent class growth analysis identified two classes. Adolescents in the first class reported high levels of digital flourishing, which remained stable over time, whereas those in the second class reported low levels of digital flourishing with decreased self-control over time. Autonomy-supportive restrictive, autonomy-supportive active, and controlling active parental mediation styles, together with high parental digital skills, predicted adolescents' belongingness to the (more digitally flourishing) first class.

Learn ENERGY MEDICINE

"Energy medicine is the next great frontier in medicine!"
– Memhet Oz, M.D., Columbia Medical School (speaking on Oprah)

Study the user-friendly yet sophisticated approach to energy medicine developed by Donna Eden

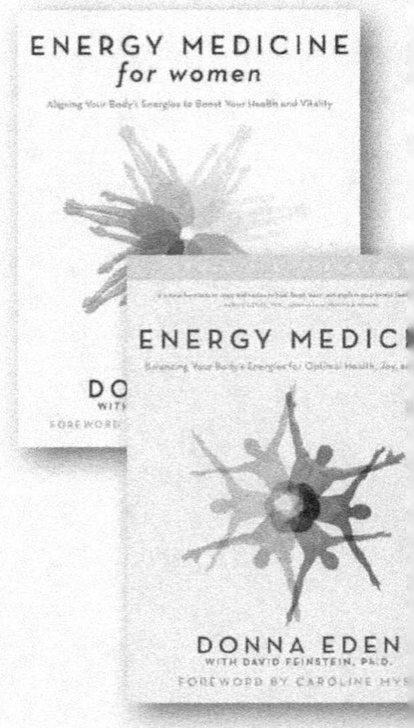

- To stay healthier, help overcome illness and pain, and live with greater vitality and joy
- For medical professionals to bring to their health care services
- A career for the future – available now!

"Donna Eden's body energy work is perhaps the m brilliant, comprehensive, and effective system in th genre that I have ever seen." **–Jean Houston, Ph.D.**

"Some people have a healing presence that makes us—and our immune systems—better than before. Donna Eden is one of those rare healers."
—Gloria Steinem

"Donna Eden is one of the most joyous and effective pioneers in the rapidly expanding and vitally important frontier called energy medicine."
—Christiane Northrup, M.D.

VISIT
www.LearnEnergyMedicine.cor
for more information about:

- Donna's books, DVDs, and other learning resources
- Local study groups
- Local classes and individual sessions with Donna's top certified practitioners
- Classes with Donna
- Enrolling in the comprehensive 2 Ye Basic Eden Energy Medicine Certificati Program plus furthe advanced study.

www.ingramcontent.com/pod-product-compliance
Lightning Source LLC
LaVergne TN
LVHW082359200926
848481LV00012B/3620
* 9 7 8 1 6 0 4 1 5 1 7 7 0 *